WARSHIPS

WARSHIPS

From Sail to the Nuclear Age

Bernard Ireland

Hamlyn
London · New York · Sydney · Toronto

Published by the Hamlyn Publishing Group Limited
London . New York . Sydney . Toronto
Astronaut House, Feltham, Middlesex, England
Copyright © 1978 the Hamlyn Publishing Group Limited

ISBN 0 600 39397 6

Printed in Spain by Printer Industria Grafica, s.a.
Deposito Legal B 10368 – 78

Contents

Preface

A letter from the Duke of Wellington once contained an apology for its length, which was due to its writer 'not having time to write a shorter one'. Faced with the problem of compressing the long development of the warship within the compass of one book, an author can fully understand the paradox. The purpose of this book is to describe the warship's evolution rather than the social history which moulded it, but, nevertheless, events need to be included. Man's perpetual warring is not just the backdrop against which the warship can be admired in isolation. It forms the mould from which it springs and only the searching tests of battle can reveal a ship's design strengths and its weaknesses. They are the forces of its evolution.

Background then, leavens what would be rather heavy factual fare but still there are so many names involved, so many incidents, that it must be hoped that the reader will be fired to refer to more detailed works covering this aspect. If he is, then the book will have been well worthwhile.

Bernard Ireland

The Beginnings
the Mediterranean

So what is a warship? Basically, it is a ship used by one state to protect its interests or to further its aims against those of another state, by force if necessary. If this sounds rather vague it is because there can never be a precise definition; warships, like the devil, come in many forms. We are accustomed these days to the multi-function, multi-system ship of immense destructive potential. Here, the crew are an auxiliary to the ship, are there to operate it and to service it, but the power remains with the ship. It was not always thus as in the beginning the roles were reversed. The only weapons used were side arms and these could injure only the enemy crew, not their ship. Fighting was by boarding, followed by man-to-man combat. The ship, therefore, was only the auxiliary and was either scuttled, destroyed by fire or carried off as the victor's booty.

The historian has been dealt a rather weak hand by contemporary records and has to reconstruct the very early ships from a blend of drawing, carving and description, making allowance for strange perspectives and exaggerations and blending-in a modicum of his own experience of what makes a ship go.

Civilisations, as we know them, grew up around the Fertile Crescent and spread to the Middle East. War was an honourable pastime and, as the great powers were land powers, it was conducted by men marching endless miles along land routes. These avoided or followed the great water obstacles formed by the seas, but the great leader is the one who does the unpredictable; he crosses an 'impossible'

mountain or jungle to attack from an unexpected quarter. One such, whose name and campaign are now forgotten, took his army across a water barrier. To ferry his men and horses, his transport and materials, he used what must by definition have been the world's first warships.

They may well have been rafts for the first known representation of a raft-like boat is from about 3,500 BC when Menes the Fighter was busy trying to become Pharaoh of Lower Egypt as well as Upper. A low relief shows a sharply sheered craft with pronounced stem- and stern-posts and she has a rudimentary cabin with a plaited roof and no mast, so was probably paddled. Her length was anything between 30 and 50 feet and she was totally unwarlike but, being a common type on the Nile,

This bowl from the 5th century BC portrays a Greek merchantman but demonstrates that oars were auxiliary to sail propulsion at this time. The many braces to control the long yard are evident, as well as halyards and backstays.

must have ferried many an expedition. Constructional details are not clear but she almost certainly consisted of bundles of papyrus reed bound into shape, even as is done in South America today.

In a treeless land such as Egypt, good lengths of timber were almost unknown, with the local acacia and sycamore yielding only short pieces of knotty wood. Boats were built for sea-going by keying together such pieces and, to give the whole some longitudinal strength, linking stem to stern with an enormous, vulnerable hogging truss. Lateral

top
A model of the Hatshepsut craft shows the yards sent down. Except for the hypothetical mast step, it would seem to agree in detail.

above
This Phoenician bireme is clearly little more than a powered ram. The outriggers project from a slender hull and support the oarsmen, above whose heads run the fore-and-aft fighting bridge for the soldiers embarked.

lengths, so this and their boat-building expertise was capitalised on by the more aggressive Egyptians. Their boats increased in size, as did their prowess and, by about 1,500 BC, Hatshepsut made her famous expedition to Punt, probably near Guardafui, the Horn of Africa. Her purpose was probably commercial but demonstrates that this land-orientated people could now take to the sea and, inevitably, we shortly afterwards find the first craft designed for war.

Rameses III, the greatest of the warring Pharaohs, built craft that were noticably slimmer than the portly traders and had a dozen oarsmen each side, protected by high bulwarks. The square sail was hung from a pole mast that had at the top what was probably a look-out's basket. What marked her out was the keel, not curving upwards into a stempost, but continuing aggressively forward in a beak, terminated by a carved animal head. It is debatable whether this was used as a ram or as a means of carving through the bank of oars of an adversary, destroying his manoeuvrability so that he could be boarded.

Here we see the ancestor of the Galley and with it Rameses defeated the Sea Peoples, an alliance probably led by the Phoenicians, whose interests were not always confined to trade.

Owing to the availability of good timber there, the parallel development of the ship in Crete and the Northern Mediterranean had following different lines. Early, simple dugouts had their seaworthiness improved by the addition of planks laid edge-to-edge, carvel fashion, increasing their freeboard and stability by the use of outriggers. The direct descendants of these were known before the time of Homer and took his heroes to the Trojan Wars.

However, ship developments were geared primarily to the day-to-day business of making a living and it is mainly of the trading ship that we find in surviving records. But, soon after the Mediterranean area inspired Rameses' fighting ships, it produced a real innovation, the Bireme. Where it could be

strength was added by the adoption of cross beams and the whole was designed to be rowed, although a bipod mast, hinged at the foot, could be raised to spread a square sail in a following wind. By 3,000 BC such a craft was sailing up the Levant coast and had probably crossed to Crete. Contact was made with the Phoenicians, natural seafarers of high business acumen who, unfortunately, left few records. One of the great advantages the Phoenicians had was the availability of timber in great

argued that a ship with a single bank of oars could be used for trade or war, the double-banked craft was purely for offence. Most of its capacity was taken up by oarsmen in two rows, one above the other on either side, each of a dozen men. The lower oars were worked through small ports in the wales, whilst the upper oarsmen were on a thwart outboard of their compatriots and rowing over an outrigger. Running the full length of the ship was a fighting bridge to allow rapid movement to the soldiers that were carried – they did the fighting, not the oarsmen, whose job it was to fling the slender craft against that of the enemy. The beak was now clearly meant for ramming, with the tremendous resultant shocks from similar attacks by an enemy being absorbed by a craft properly framed with ribs, beams and longitudinals. A low, collapsible mast could spread a square sail on a yard of almost twice its length. This could be braced over a wide angle but was little use in anything but a following wind. Its low height underlined the inherent tenderness of the craft. If the wind freshened unacceptably, it could not be shortened, only brailed up to the yard and lowered complete.

This type of warship was common about the seventh century BC to the Greeks, Phoenicians and Assyrians but gave pride of place fairly quickly to the Trireme. The devotees of more power reasoned that more rowers behind a ram would have more lethal results and succeeded in accommodating three banks of oars per side. How it was done it is still not certain, but three 'layers' would have resulted in the upper oars being unacceptably long and heavy, and the rowers were probably seated on the same level in a complex layout to avoid fouling. Even so the inboard rank must have handled very long sweeps, so there may have been two rowers to each of them. All oars ran through ports in a very substantial outrigger, which transmitted the thrust to the hull. The trireme of the fifth century BC was probably 130 feet in length, with a covered fore-and-aft bridge now affording

This representation of Greek fire in use offers little exact information on the methods employed.

protection to the crew. Probably this type of ship was in the minority in a fleet, acting as the heavy back-up to the more handy squadrons of biremes.

The ram was effectively used at Salamis in 480 BC, although the standard boarding tactics still decided the day. Here, the numerically superior Persians were lured through a narrow channel and taken in the flank as they emerged. The fight inevitably degenerated into a mêlée but the Greeks won because the Persians were unable to deploy their larger numbers.

Boarding was a hit-and-miss affair and good ship design counted for little; a barge could take a trireme if it grappled her. Similarly, successful ramming was hazardous, probably sinking the rammer as often as the rammed. So men began considering other more cost-effective methods of defeating the enemy by sinking his ship rather than by killing the crew. Catapults, or ballistae, were well known but were lacking in power, their bolts and stone missiles only complementing the archers' shafts. The tough hide of a ship was left unscathed.

One answer was fire. Years of experiment produced the fabulous 'Greek Fire', fabulous advisedly, for it was probably never as good as legend would have us believe.

It certainly burned fiercely, resisting water and gravely threatening the highly flammable hulls of the time. However, it was only catapulted with difficulty and must have been dangerous equally to friend or foe. Thus it became accepted practice to suspend a blazing pot at the end of a long, hinged spar in the bows of a ship and to manoeuvre so as to deposit it on the enemy's deck. He then had to try extinguishing it either by sand or with vinegar – or the rower's wine ration.

The ram continued to be the accepted weapon as is evidenced by many references to quad- and quinquiremes. These ships could not have had four or five banks of oars as the whole would have been impossibly cumbersome. Almost certainly the names used must have referred to the number of ranks of rowers, and was a measure of power in the days before 'horse-power' had been invented. The large body of men in such a ship required a larger hull, now roofed over with a full-width fighting deck. The oarsmen could see out only through their narrow ports and stood little chance if the ship was sunk. This was a type of warship favoured by the Romans.

A series of wars against Carthage really forced Rome – very much a land power – into mounting and supporting a campaign by sea. The Carthaginians were adept at this form of warfare but the Romans were always ready to learn. Their standard, and rather uninspired, tactic of smashing their opponent's centre ranks relied on their superb discipline and resolution, but laid them open to defeat when faced with a tactician versed in the arts of outflanking and encircling. Persistance paid off, however, underlining the dictum that 'a good big 'un will always beat a good little 'un' and, with the fall of Carthage about 150 BC, Rome was undisputed master of the Mediterranean and much of its littoral.

The trireme of the times was propelled by 170 oars and the crew of 200 included spare oarsmen and sailing crew. In addition, 80 marines were carried for actual combat. It is probable that the fabled quinquireme had no more

oars, but just two men on each of the two inside positions and one on the outer, with his shorter oar mounted inboard and at a lower level.

Probably inspired by captured biremes, the Romans produced an improved variant known as a Liburnian, which proved very effective against heavier opponents in the internecine battle of Actium in the last century BC. Subsequently, Augustus grouped the Roman fleet into four organised commands, two based on Italy and one each to police the Syrian and Egyptian waters.

Several Roman innovations are of interest. Reproductions of the time show small tower structures amidships, possibly of a temporary nature. These appear too small to have real fighting value, but could have elevated key personnel. Of more use was the introduction of a second sail, the Artemon. This was spread on a yard suspended from a steeply steeved bowsprit and assisted these unhandy sailers in going about. To achieve rapid boarding, a hinged bridge was hung from a kingpost forward, and allowed to drop over on to an enemy's deck, keeping its position there by virtue of a beak-like spike which pierced the planking and

gave the device its name of Corvus, or Raven.

Caesar at this time was subjugating Gaul and had great trouble with the Veneti, the inhabitants of what is now Brittany. They constructed fortresses on each headland and relied upon their substantial fleet for communication. Caesar, having no luck by land, had a fleet built locally on the Loire. Despite the unfamiliar tidal range and heavy seas he sought battle and eventually intercepted the main body of the Gauls. Caesar records how his Roman-style ships were at a disadvantage against the enemy's craft which were designed for sailing rather than rowing. They had flat bottom sections enabling them to escape into inlets and 'take the beach' and they had high sides, making them difficult to board. The Roman fleet had almost lost them when a calm gave their rowing galleys the advantage. Grappling hooks cleared the Veneti's standing rigging and brought down their masts; boarding completed the operation. Beyond the decisive effect that it had on the campaign, this battle was significant for the fact that southern warships had met those of the north for the first time. And the latter were of an entirely different breed.

This representation of a Greek galley of the 4th century BC shows the typical narrow-gutted appearance of a rowed warship. Note the double steering oars and the crutch for accepting the mast when lowered.

Developments
the North

The ships of the northern seas developed for much the same reasons as those of the southern. Men needed to fish and they needed transport in a wheel-less, roadless age. Again they used materials that were to hand, but having little contact between peoples, progress was along different lines in different places. In place of the reed, they had the animal hide which, unlike reed bundles, had no inherent rigidity. It was, therefore, stitched by thongs to a pliable frame and, although too fragile to be sailed, such boats could easily be taken ashore and inverted for shelter. Thus, the principles of framing were grasped early, which is confirmed by numerous Scandinavian drawings of before 1,000 BC. These also show a common feature of a forward end terminating in two horns, one of these being a skid-like projection to what appears to be a keel. This member was probably introduced as a runner to take the wear of constant dragging up stony beaches, but was soon strengthened and became the backbone of the whole frame. Added incentive to improvement in boat design was given by the northern climate. The Mediterranean was not a sea to trifle with, but at least it was warm. A ducking in northern waters often spelt death from exposure.

Seakeeping qualities were allied to size and, the hide cladding being an obvious limitation, the next step was to clad in timber, cut laboriously into thin planks by hand. The earliest known example of this was the remains of a boat of the third century BC near the Alssund, in Denmark. She had been

a 43-footer and built by somebody familiar with hide construction, for the five strakes of timber on each side had been stitched to the frame members. Another feature distinguished most northern craft from their southern contemporaries. Compared with the Mediterranean's edge-to-edge carvel construction, they were made clinker-style with overlapping planking, which had to be built inverted with the garboard strakes first fitted along the flat keel and each successive strake lapping it like tiles on a

These Bronze Age rock paintings from Sweden show the keeled construction of boats, continued forward to a horned projection to ease the task of running the boat up a beach. The familiar high stern and stern-posts are also apparent, capped with carved animal heads or, possibly, skulls.

roof. This construction made for a flexible boat that 'gave' in the steep seas of the shallow Baltic and North Seas.

The Alssund boat was probably rowed but the solid-framed design allowed for easy enlargement and her successors were sailing within a century. Their double-horned ends were now faired neatly into high, scarphed-on stem and stern posts, features noted by the Romans half a century before Caesar's defeat of the Veneti.

We now see emerging the famous 'longship', synonymous with the Norsemen, whose depredations made them the scourge of anything civilised and who could handle boats as none before them and few since. In the small communities of the north a multiplicity of craft were developed, all conforming to similar rules. Fighting ships and traders alike featured the graceful high-ended hull, steered by an oar on the starboard ('steer-board') quarter. The cargo-carrier had somewhat fuller lines and a further interesting difference lay in the transverse beams. In the trader, these took the form of thwarts for the rowers but the warship had true beams, set a little lower, and decked over, leaving a clear run obstructed only by a complex step which permitted the mast to be lowered. This mast carried a yard spreading a large square sail. This was not striped, as in popular renderings, but reinforced diagonally with leather strips to prevent the hand-woven fabric from bagging hopelessly out of shape.

This type of ship, functional but of extreme beauty, formed the basis of every design for the next millennium. They lacked every creature comfort but were used to penetrate ever farther into unknown seas. Winter seagoing was bleak in the extreme but, with coming of spring, shore communities within reach of the fierce northern sailors looked fearfully to sea at the commencement of the raiding season.

An immense advantage of the longship's sailing qualities was that rowing was kept to a minimum. Separate rowing and fighting crews were, therefore, not required as in the Mediterranean and the ships had a greater range on the stores which could be carried, a range really limited only by the endurance of the crew itself.

From the time of Christ to the Norman Invasion, all northern warships were merely refinements of the longship. These ranged from the 100-footer with 40 oars to one related in the Sagas as having belonged to Canute, which was

below
This commemorative stone from the Swedish island of Götland shows Vikings about their usual pursuits and also, more interestingly, the diagonal reinforcements of the sails continued in a complicated series of bridles.

below, right
Broken but beautiful, the Oseberg ship is here seen in 1904 before reclamation. Even in this condition the details of her construction and the excellence of craftsmanship are clear.

250 feet long and propelled by 120 oars (and probably some imagination!) The very basic rigging would be familiar to today's seamen, with a single-section mast stepped into a block and supported by two backstays, adjusted by wooden deadeyes. The heavy yard and sail were raised smoothly on parrels by a halyard rove through a block, sometimes paired for mechanical advantage. For sailing, the yard was trimmed by braces and the sail could be boomed out like today's spinnaker. Anchor cable was fabricated from iron links, conferring greater weight and hence holding power. These were ships designed for sailing; in the north the winds they were reliable and in conditions that demanded seaworthiness, though the lack of instant oar-power never favoured the ram.

During the long sleep of the Dark Ages, the raiders from the North came and went at will. Some settled in more equable climates and brought their skills with them. They, in turn, had need to build to defend themselves against further predators and a Saxon variant of the longship developed. With better leadership and better ships the English (if such they can be called) felt able, by the ninth century, to challenge the raiding Danish squadrons. Credit for this, much embroidered with myth, was given to King Alfred and, for the first time, we read of successes by Saxon ships 'twice as long and shaped like neither Friesian nor Dane'. By the year AD 1,000 we had Ethelred levying taxes to finance warship building but control of the country was not vested wholly in the Crown for Edward (the Confessor) had to meet a naval challenge from the dissident Earl Godwin. But the turbulence of England's internal affairs came to an abrupt end with the appearance of a battle fleet off the East Sussex coast. The year was 1066. The fleet was that of William of Normandy.

King Harold's English fleet was well concentrated along the coast at Sandwich but for some reason, possibly a brisk south-westerly wind, did not oppose history's first large-scale amphibious landing from a recorded 700 ships. The Bayeux tapestry records the event accurately, together with the build-up to the invasion and the well-known results. The ships are depicted in detail and show little improvement over the original longship. Saxon ships differ from Norman in not having a continuous line of rowing ports, which suggests that they may have been

decked amidships. William's ship carries an identifying device, either standard or lantern, at the mast-head.

Although William 'burned his boats' in an interesting historical precedent, he soon found the need of a fleet and set about reconstruction. One method that he adopted was the granting of certain privileges to five towns in return for their financing a standing force for use on demand by the Crown. Thus were the Cinque Ports created, in 1078.

Little progress was made with the establishment of a regular fleet, although by the end of the twelfth century, Henry II felt strong enough to claim sovereignty over 'British Seas'. He was followed by Richard I, who went crusading so much as to almost totally exclude his true role of ruling the kingdom. Nevertheless, it was he who returned Caesar's compliment by taking a sizable Anglo-Aquitaine

The custom of burying great leaders with their ship has preserved several Norse craft, and the extreme beauty of the Oseberg ship is complemented by its setting in the Oslo Folk museum.

An Anglo-French skirmish on St. Bartholomew's Day, 1217. The English (blessed by their bishops) are engaged in grappling and boarding. Slings and arrows are used at longer range for putting oil-pots aboard the enemy.

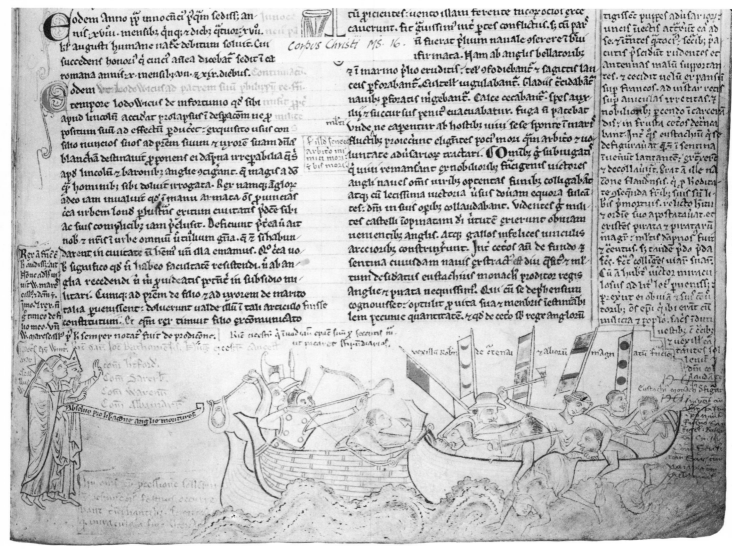

fleet into the Mediterranean. His ships were mostly traders pressed into official service, which was not as risky as it sounds, for the warship scarcely differed in detail from the merchantman at this time and almost certainly reverted to trading in times of peace. Contemporary representations show the disappearance of the rowing port and the ships themselves much beamier, with a still-pronounced sheer but lacking high end posts. Some mounted temporary fore-and-aftercastles for use in close combat and had a look-out's basket aloft. The

bowsprit had re-appeared, but only to give a better lead to the sheets, and the vulnerable steering-oar was yielding to proper rudders. Overall, they were probably inferior sailers to the Viking ships, but more robust.

In the eastern Mediterranean this crusading fleet encountered what the chroniclers describe as a 'great Saracen ship', 'three masted' and having '1,500' men. The sheer size of this craft defied attempts to take her, liquid Greek fire was ejected from special tubes, and her high freeboard prevented boarding. She

eventually succumbed to a mass ramming, which suggests that galleys formed part of Richard's fleet. This 'great ship' was probably the first recorded Dromon, a large bireme galley, rigged with a lateen sail. The lateen rig was new to Northern seamen and had its origins much further east. From its triangular form the fore-and-aft rigs developed, with their improved performances to windward.

A powerful political influence of that time was the Hansa League, a federation of North European trad-

This model of a 13th century Englishman from the Cinque Ports is a rather literal adaption from the Dover Seal. The steering oar, still used, is shown on the port side. The large castles and top are of interest, as is the grapnel forward.

ing towns which evolved the famous Cog, a stout oaken barrel of a ship with capacious cargo space, straighter ends than previously for sailing to windward, and a shallow draught for penetrating well up-river. Rudders and end-castles were now quite general, but the clumsy type of square sail had been improved only to the extent that it could be shortened by reef-points or increased in size by lacing a strip of canvas called a 'bonnet' to the bottom. Another feature was a

right, top
A Hansa cog on the seal of the Baltic town of Stralsund, 1329. The stern rudder was, by this time, about 150 years old. The aftercastle has become part of the main hull but the forecastle somewhat stylised.

right, lower
An early 13th century seal of the Hansa City of Lübeck shows how the basic Norse ship has not yet been developed.

bowsprit, again for improving the run of the sheets, but often depicted with a grapnel suspended from the upper end. This implement is a reminder of the dual nature of the craft and was used for grappling an enemy in time of war.

King John, who succeeded Richard to the English throne, proved a failure in many ways but understood the value of seapower sufficiently to meet a threat from France by building up the fleet. The only battle of note was fought at Damme in 1213. Rudimentary tactics were used by the English in deliberately seeking the weather gauge and sweeping down upon their enemy, sending out clouds of powdered quicklime. The half-blinded French succumbed quickly to the determined boarding which followed. Unethical it may have been, but it was the first of many examples that demonstrate that unorthodoxy can well carry the day.

Relations between England and France had degenerated by now into an almost permanent state of war. Often it was undeclared and consisted of quarrels between various towns or factions. We see at the turn of the thirteenth century the issue of the first 'Letters of Marque', documents which, over the years, became debased into little more than licences for legalised piracy in the name of 'privateering'. In 1338 Edward II put 40,000 men ashore in Flanders from an invasion force of about 500 ships. His satisfaction was short-lived, however, as the French fleet, instead of attacking this force, took advantage of its preoccupation and sacked several English south-coast towns with impunity. Vengeance was two years a-coming but fell on a French force at Sluys. The English fleet, diverted from another invasion force, found them close inshore and lashed together for mutual protection. Pinned down by the English longbowmen, they were boarded and carried, in spite of their use of baskets-full of stones dropped from aloft. This form of weapon was original but completely surpassed by a noisy acquisition of the English. The gun had arrived.

'. . . and has come to Pevensey.' The
inscription on this part of the Bayeux
Tapestry refers to the best-recorded of
history's early amphibious landings.
Note how the knights travel in separate
ships to their horses (which could have
caused severe logistic problems had the
landing been vigorously opposed!).

bottom
A detail from Froissart's *Chronicles* shows
an attack on the Earl of Pembroke's
ship outside La Rochelle in the late 14th
century. Grappling and boarding was
the order of the day.

The Gun
the Start of a Revolution

Even in 1340 the gun was, of course, nothing new; missiles had been ejected explosively from barrels for about two centuries. Quite large cast bronze guns existed ashore but, shipboard, they tended to be small, swivel-mounted pieces. Although we know of injuries to personnel being sustained by gunfire in a Baltic skirmish about this time, the effect was psychological rather than practical. The guns were inaccurate, short-ranged, and more likely to kill the gunner than his target. As the English longbowman could still pin a man to the deck at 130 yards, it was hardly a serious contender.

The armament of the Venetian and Genoese galleys had advanced rather more quickly with heavy, stone-firing bombards mounted forward. The presence of oars down each side limited the siting of guns to the ends of the ship, usually forward. This severe limitation dogged the galley throughout its history and enforced the head-on, line-abreast attack that became its trademark.

The average English ship, modelled on those of the Hansa, now took another step forward using influence from Spain. This latter country was unwise enough to ally herself with France in the latest dispute against the English who, hearing of a loaded Flota heading down-channel for home, found the taste for plunder over-whelming and a squadron, under the King himself, fell upon it. The Castilians had larger hulls and a larger sail area and the English, unable to board by conventional means, took them by the simple expedient of ramming them, losing many of their own ships in the process. However, the value of the captured ships transcended that of

This Dutch painting of *Portuguese carracks off a rocky coast* dates from 1520–30 and shows a large armed carrack, possibly the *Santa Catarina do Monte Sinai*. Notable points are the many decks, four masts, bellying courses controlled by relieving tackles and the foremast crossed for a topsail.

right
This battle off Gibraltar in 1607 shows the wide range of ships in the average battle fleet and the general mêlée typical of the time. Note how the Dutch ships have kept their fore-courses set to maintain steerage way.

below
16th century falconets. These breech-loaders threw a 2-pound ball and were members of a large family of 'murdering pieces', swivel-mounted on the bulwarks, and used as anti-personnel weapons.

right, lower
An expedition by Philip II to the Azores. This contemporary impression of Spanish warships shows their high freeboard and general 'un-handy' appearance when compared with an Englishman.

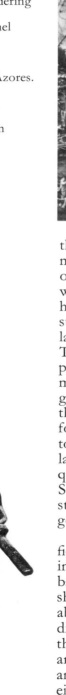

their cargoes, for they became the model for an important new breed of ship, the Carrack. This vessel was of Mediterranean origin and had certain local characteristics, such as carvel planking and a lateen sail on a small mizzen mast. This sail provided a new facility in putting about, which complemented the main driving force still generated by a large square sail on the mainmast. A bowsprit and forecastle were standard features, together with an integral aftercastle large enough to be termed a raised quarterdeck. A rudder – new to the South – was hung on to the bluff stern. Her carrying capacity was good and she was an instant success.

The basic design had been modified by the mid-fifteenth century to include a foremast the better to balance the effect of the mizzen. A shorter half-deck had been added above the quarterdeck, creating a distinct 'waist' between that and the the forecastle. This low centre area was vulnerable to boarding and could be swept by fire from either castle but it was there for a very real purpose. It was a gundeck. The carrack was large and beamy enough to carry four or five large guns on either broadside, mounted on fixed carriages and firing over a low bulwark. They needed to be carried low because of their weight.

Cast guns of this size were expensive and unreliable, and the common method of construction was to fabricate them from a cylinder made of iron strips laid parallel around formers and hammer-welded together with iron hoops. All gaps were then sealed with lead, leaving both ends open. The ball and its charge were loaded into a breech casting which was then secured to the barrel for firing. A variation on this method was to bolt together a series of similar cast tubes with flanged ends.

In 1485, as the European renaissance dawned, Henry VII came to the English throne. He began not only the Tudor dynasty but also a new era for the navy, establishing it as a regular force. The first drydock was built at Portsmouth so that the great ships could be properly repaired without having to careen them on a hard.

At the turn of the sixteenth century a battle of far-reaching consequence was fought in the Indian Ocean when an exploring squadron of Portuguese ships under da Gama were attacked by a large and varied fleet of Arab craft. The latter, being lateen-rigged dhows, were of superior manoeuvrability to the carracks but were armed only with a few short-barrelled bombards that lobbed

stone balls with high trajectories. da Gama's ships were armed with long-pieces along the broadside. By keeping a disciplined line of battle, they gave each other mutual protection from boarding, and were able to defeat the enemy at a safe range. The advantages of the stand-off action were plain to see.

The Venetians were among the greatest of the trading powers of these times and suffered greatly from Mediterranean piracy. As a direct result, their carracks were developed to carry broadsides of up to 20 guns. A squared-off transom allowed stern chasers to be mounted and above, against the taffrail, they added a fourth mast, termed the Bonaventure Mizzen. It was too small to be of practical use and required a projecting bumpkin to spread its sail. In this ship lay the basis of what was to become the English Galleon.

Henry VIII, himself larger than life, was impressed by big ships with big guns and pursued their construction with a ruthless energy. A Scottish ship of the time, inspired the Henri Grâce à Dieu, soon immortalised as the *Great Harry*. She was of the new 'race-built' type and, although her impressive inventory of 250 guns included only 20 'heavies', they really were designed to sink an opponent. The Cannon

25

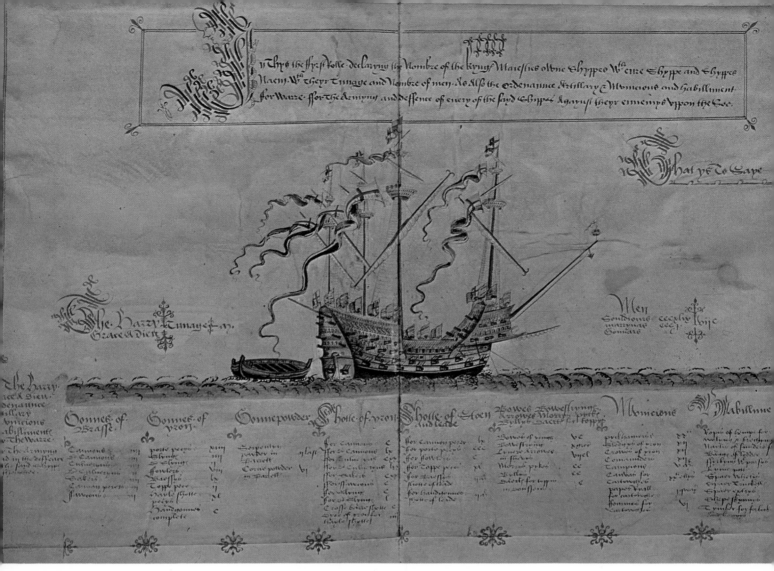

This contemporary drawing of the *Henry Grâce à Dieu* and her establishment is from the Anthony Rolls of 1546. The ship, a nominal 80-gunner, was built on the Thames in 1514, rebuilt at Portsmouth in 1539, and destroyed by fire in 1553 after having been renamed *Edward*.

Royal, with its carriage, weighed nearly four tons and fired a 68-pound iron ball. Only the introduction of the gun-port (probably from France) enabled these to be mounted low enough to maintain acceptable stability of the ship. In bad weather the guns could be run-in and the ports secured. The close-ranged ship-smashing properties of the Cannon Royal were complemented by those of the Culverin, much used as bow-chasers and throwing an 18-pound shot a distance of a mile and a half.

The period also saw the introduction of the Galleass. The idea was for a galleon with a single bank of oars for manoeuvrability in wind-less conditions and was attractive but, like most compromises, it fell short of expectations. At one stage, the ratio of galleasses to 'shyppes' was 15 to 20 but it rapidly lost popularity, and by the end of Henry VIII's reign had almost disappeared from the navy list. It persisted in other fleets, notably in the Baltic.

Hostilities with France continued and the French adopted a 'fleet-in-being' approach, remaining in port and forcing the English to come to them. The result was the creation of the cutting-out expedition and a marked drop in French morale and efficiency due to inactivity. More significantly, the English fleet assumed the role of attacker; it found it to its taste, it developed it, it refined it – and it never lost it.

Although a spent force in the North, the rowed warship was still of importance in the Mediterranean. In 1571, at Lepanto, Don John of Austria, with a combined Christian fleet, smashed the Turkish domination of the area. It was a battle of rowed warships, all of them being galleys with the exception of six Christian galleasses, whose broadside fire proved decisive.

With the accession of Elizabeth I as Queen of England a new holy war began with her sister, of another faith, pretending to the throne, actively supported by Spain. The two countries were now great rivals in the carving up of newly discovered lands and Spain was anxious to see the downfall of England. She, however, was having difficulty in suppressing a revolt in the Low Countries, then held in her thrall and this revolt was actively supported by Elizabeth. In the likelihood of a war against a maritime power, the English fleet was in a dangerously run-down condition, but was built up by Elizabeth with the encouragement of the 'gentleman adventurers'. By putting up money from the public

26

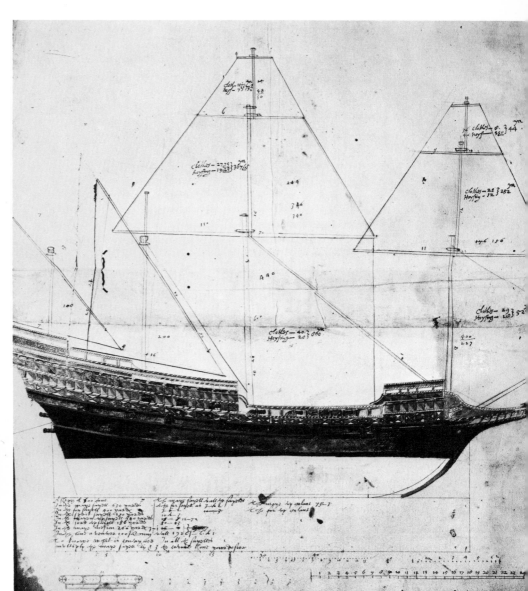

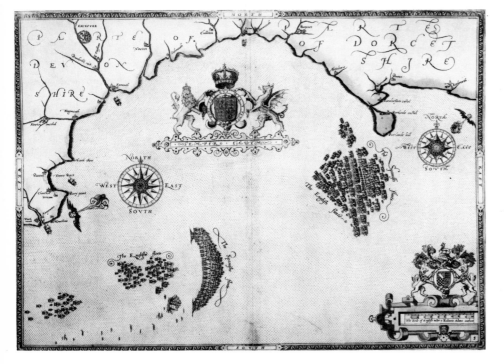

above
An English race-built ship of the Armada period in a draught by the master-shipwright Matthew Baker. The main battery is mounted low and a bonaventure mizzenmast shipped.

left, above
The 1588 Armada medal rightly gives credit to the weather, rather than English tactics, for the virtual annihilation of the Spanish fleet.

left
A 1590 map by Adam Ryther shows clearly how the disciplined, crescent-shaped formation of the Armada off the Devon coast kept the English fleet at a distance. On relaxing their formation off Portland they lost the benefit of mutual covering fire and were closed by the faster English.

27

The fireship has been much over-rated by legend but could cause real panic when sailed into an anchored fleet, as was done to the Spanish Armada by the English off Gravelines.

purse to assist in the fitting-out of their expeditions, she gained more from shares in the prizes which they took and established a nucleus of purpose-built ships and highly experienced crews under captains whose names have become legends.

Most of this maritime war was against commercial vessels but a prophetic battle was fought off the Azores in 1582 by an Anglo-French squadron, which defeated an inferior Spanish force by line-of-battle tactics and the gun, rather than by resorting to boarding. Some English commanders, particularly Hawkins, treated gunnery as a science. They believed in the culverin as a means of out-ranging their opponents and, having thus at least partly crippled them, closing to finish the job with heavier guns or by boarding. The latter method

was wasteful of manpower but popular if there was any prospect of booty.

Spain's only hope for neutralising the English threat lay in invasion. This was well understood by the English – and feared. As the force to accomplish this would need to be conveyed by sea, a *guerre de course* developed against the storeships engaged in the transport of materials. By the time the 'enterprise' eventually sailed in 1588 it was short of all vital supplies. About half the 130-odd ships were warships, little larger than the English ships but much higher in the hull and less handy. They were crammed with fighting men for the invasion, but, as the English had no intention of boarding, they were a liability in action. All the way up-Channel they kept rigid formation and the English fleet had little luck, but they anchored that night in Calais and were attacked by English fireships. These rather over-rated craft created the desired panic and forced the Spaniards to sea, where they

were dealt with piecemeal in rapidly deteriorating weather. Whilst the the English could replenish ammunition from home bases, their opponents could not, and any coherence in their force was broken, leaving individual ships the daunting task of circumnavigating the British Isles to return to Spain. Few made it.

The Armada medal that was struck bears the inscription 'God blew and they were scattered' and this really sums up an untidy action. The English could outmanoeuvre their lofty opponents but their long-range culverins were too light to sink them. Most were lost to the weather.

If proof were needed that close-ranged heavy cannon fire was necessary to sink a ship it came three years later when Grenville's *Revenge* tangled with no less than 53 Spanish ships. They boarded and eventually took her by sheer weight of numbers, but had to close to do so. They lost probably four ships as a result of point blank broadside gunfire, and up to 16 more suc-

left
At Lepanto in 1571, the Turkish domination of the Eastern Mediterranean was broken by a combined Christian fleet. Over 300 galleys were involved on each side, but the Christians also had six galleasses (visible right, middle distance) whose broadside fire was probably decisive.

below
Sir Richard Grenville will always be remembered for the heroic resistance of his *Revenge* in action with 53 Spanish warships in 1591. His heavy broadside fire caused vast damage to the Spaniards, whose fleet was largely of galleys and dependent upon boarding. *Revenge* was boarded and taken only after her powder was exhausted.

cumbed to the damage they had sustained in a severe storm that followed.

As if to underline the ineffectiveness of the galley in comparison to the galleon the Spanish, in 1602, were unwise enough to send a squadron of them up to the Netherlands. They were intercepted in a strong blow by an Anglo-Dutch force and destroyed, not only by gunnery but also by ramming – a neat reversal on the galley's usual tactics.

Peace with Spain followed soon after Elizabeth's death in 1603, but a new rivalry sprang up with England's late ally, the Dutch, who were natural seamen, traders and colonisers.

Influenced by the lessons of both the Armada and the *Revenge* actions, designers now went for powerfully armed ships. 'Race-building' was abandoned as two deckers made way for ships with ever-longer after half decks, which eventually formed a complete third gun deck. The outstanding example of this new breed was the 56-gun *Prince Royal* of 1610, twice the size of the earlier *Revenge*. She was a product of that fine, but controversial Master Shipwright, Phineas Pett. She retained the rather useless bonaventure mizzen but did not have the equally pointless small mast spreading a square sail and stepped on the bowsprit that was coming into vogue.

Typically, a large ship of the

An° · DNI · 1571 · ÆTATIS · SVÆ · 29 ·

ir Richard Granville, killed
a sea-fight near the Azores.

below
Built at Woolwich in 1655, the 80-gun *Naseby* was renamed *Royal Charles* on the Restoration in 1660. Seven years later she was taken by de Ruyter in the Medway.

bottom
The lower gun-deck of the 64-gun Swedish *Wasa*, seen soon after her salvage. The guns are missing from their carriages but the heavy framing of the ship is striking. Note the hazard to watertight integrity caused by the hatches and gratings along the centre line.

time carried in addition a square sail below the bowsprit (after the fashion of the Roman artemon) to assist it in going about. She spread topsails on the three forward masts including one above the lateen mizzen. Topgallants had been introduced on fore- and mainmasts only. This great spread of canvas was carried above a varnished hull with gilded and painted ornamentation along the upper gundeck and around the after end.

The pace-setting British Navy was being closely rivalled abroad however, with the Dutch building ships with up to 60 guns for the nascent French Navy. The Swedish 64-gun *Wasa* was lost in 1628 for much the same reason as many before and after – many guns meant that the lowest range of gunports was too close to the waterline. And the guns at this level were of no use in any sort of a breeze because, if the ports were left open, the ship could flood rapidly in a squall.

In 1637, Phineas Pett and his son produced the legendary *Sovereign of the Seas* for their new patron, Charles I. She was incredible for her time, a full three-decker, triple-planked and carrying 104 large guns of various sizes. In addition, there were more ports 'within-board for murdering pieces', a reminder that boarding was still to be expected. She was a three-master, spreading royals above her topgallants, and the extravagance of her decoration became something of a scandal. She was, nevertheless, very well built and the decoration was later cut down. She saw much action during her 50-year career, which was terminated by fire.

The seething undercurrents of Anglo-Dutch rivalry lapsed for a time mainly through Britain's internal preoccupations with the Civil War. Then Parliament, having established supremacy, set about rebuilding the fleet which had been considerably reduced by the defection of 25 ships. They succeeded in putting it in shape in time for the first Anglo-Dutch War of 1652. This was a new type of sea war, the quest for supremacy of seaspace itself. Gone were the earlier comparatively minor scuffles and raids and we now saw two fleets, commanded by first-rate seamen, locked in a trial of strength. But their more disciplined approach was responsible for that greatest loser of actions, that greatest stultifier of initiative, the Line-of-Battle.

An exquisite portrait of a man and his ship – the Master Shipwright Phineas Pett and his superb *Sovereign of the Seas* of 1637. Although extravagant in her decoration, she was stoutly built and was finally burned by accident in 1696.

A rather fanciful Cornelius Vroom picture pits Spanish ships against Barbary pirates. Owing to frequent Mediterranean calms, the oared ship often had the advantage over the pure sailing vessel, and North African pirates were a problem that would take centuries to eradicate.

Maturity

the establishment of the battle fleet

The pitting of fleet against fleet demanded careful thought about tactics which would avoid the development of an untidy mêlée, where a whole squadron could perhaps be cut off and destroyed. The policy became one of mutual defence between ships, but too much stress was laid upon the avoidance of loss and too little on the encouragement of attack. Where the British had taken on a natural attacking role when faced with the French, the aggressive Dutch stance of 'keeping the sea' seemed to shake this new-found confidence somewhat. Possibly Cromwell's 'instant admirals', the Generals-at-Sea, took too much rigid military thought with them.

With broadside-armed ships it was, of course, best to sail in line ahead, leaving unobstructed firing zones on either beam. The idea had often been used before, but now it was law. The fleet was to retain formation until the strength of the opposition was broken. Only then, and with permission, could a divisional commander pursue and destroy in detail. In practice, with ships varying so much in sailing qualities, it often took so long to form the line that the chance of decisive action was lost irretrievably.

Since the Civil War, warships had been classed by 'rates' and only first to fourth rates could take their place in a line. Initially, rating was by size of complement but this was soon changed to strength of main armament. Thus, a First Rate had over 90 guns; Second, 80 to 90; Third, 50 to 80; Fourth, 38 to 50; Fifth, 18 to 38; and Sixth less than 18.

Ideas on fighting were still quite fluid. Boarding was to be encouraged only for the taking of an already beaten enemy, the British ideal being to close to 'half-cannon shot' and suddenly open fire with rapid, disciplined broadsides, aimed at smashing the hull.

The weather gauge was always sought for ease of manoeuvre and the clearance of gunsmoke. Its disadvantage was that the lowest tier of guns on the engaged side were often wave-washed and unusable. An opponent's guns, conversely, were elevated by their ship's heel away from the wind and all could be kept in action, which was probably the origin of the French preference for disabling an adversary by firing at the rigging rather than the hull. The only real variations of methods of attack provided for under the terms of the Fighting Instructions allowed the doubling of an enemy line 'under favourable circumstances' to engage the other side or – an opening for the aggressively minded – the line could steer at the enemy, break his own line, and engage the separate parts.

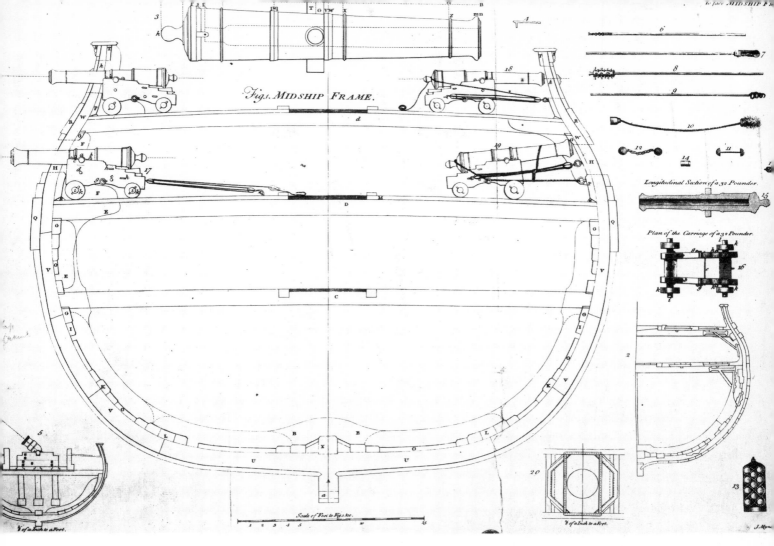

Fig.1. MIDSHIP FRAME.

Longitudinal Section of a 32 Pounder.

Plan of the Carriage of a 32 Pounder.

Scale of Feet to Fig.1 &c.

POUPE DU VAISSEAU LE DAUPHIN ROYAL
Premier Rang

above

These pages from Falconer's Marine Dictionary of 1769 show the cross-section of a wooden two-decker, with a clear insight into the use of gun tackles and breechings. The smaller details show, clockwise from upper right, gunnery implements, types of shot, details of a 32-pdr. and its carriage, another half section showing iron knees, grape shot and, lower left, a section across a bomb ketch.

left

A Spanish galley being run down by a Dutchman, 1602. Galleys were developed for the calmer Mediterranean and proved to be failures in Northern conditions.

right

Detail of the stern galleries of a Frenchman of the late 17th century. Superbly ornate but vulnerable to axial fire from an opponent.

Between 1652 and 1664, three sea wars were fought against the Dutch. To begin with the latter had the edge, but the British emerged clear victors in the end, with large commercial gains. Names like de Ruyter and Tromp, Blake and the Duke of York became household names and the nation had discovered the value of the convoy system. But the Restoration had come and an ungrateful country ran down the navy in the name of social reform.

The British three-decker of the time tended to be too fine of line and had a tendency to be 'crank' when compared with the Dutchman. The latter, plagued by shallow home waters, went for broad-beamed, shallow draughted, two-deckers which sailed much more upright in a blow. They were thus usually able to use all their guns when a British adversary was forced to close her lower gunports, nullifying the advantages of her heavier battery. The three-decker was popular with the French too, but was beamier than

33

Michael Adriaanszoon de Ruyter, born in 1607, was the greatest of the Dutch fighting admirals of the 17th century. After much action against the British, Swedes and even North African pirates, he was made Dutch Naval C-in-C in 1665. He crowned his career with the 1667 raid on the Medway, but was mortally wounded in action with the French in 1676.

origin, they began as plain ketches with the foremast taken out and the deck strengthened for a large mortar. These fired a spherical explosive shell (as opposed to solid shot) with a high trajectory, and were useful for inshore work against prepared defences. The lack of foremast gave a good field of fire but poor sailing qualities, and they soon developed an odd two-masted rig of their own, with large headsails.

In 1672 when the 'Superbe' 74 was copied, France was an ally but expanding her fleet rapidly and well under Colbert. This, predictably aroused British suspicions and war was inevitable when France supported the scheming of James II after he abdicated. The Dutch, however, were now Britain's allies as William of Orange was on the British throne. An Anglo-Dutch fleet defeated the French soundly at La Hogue in 1692 and any likelihood of another formal 'sea-war' disappeared when the French immediately adopted a *guerre-de-course* against the vulnerable English south coast shipping lanes. This was extremely effective, as they employed the fast, lugger-rigged *chasse-maree* crewed by ex-fishermen who knew the English coast well. Their object was to capture rather than sink merchant shipping, so their crews were large and their armament small, with reliance upon their fleetness to escape from naval 'cruisers'. Lying off prominent landfalls, they took trade almost at will; the navy was almost powerless and received harsh treatment from a vitriolic press. It exposed a fundamental weakness in Britain's maritime supremacy that was exploited throughout the next century of Anglo-French wars – and in the later First World War.

A brief moratorium followed the Treaty of Rijswijk in 1697 enabling both sides to rebuild. The British ships designs were still hampered by a rigid Establishment governing armament and scantlings for each rate, and were still over-gunned and poorer sailers than the French. The latter's ships were larger and more weatherly, and were able to choose their range and break off the

its British equivalent and of such superior sailing qualities that, in 1672, one was copied exactly for service with the Royal Navy (as it became known with the Restoration). If the '74' was the workhorse of the fleet the maid-of-all-work was the Frigate.

Officially, ships were still all referred to by rate but the term 'frigate' became common with both Dutch and British fleets in the late seventeenth century. Initially it meant no more than a single decker and armament varied widely.

Another ship-type to emerge at this time was the Bomb Ketch (or just 'Bomb'). Probably of French

above
1667. A Dutch Squadron under de
Ruyter suddenly descends on the
Medway and an un-mobilised British
fleet. The *Royal Charles* 80 (ex-Naseby)
was taken, and three other ships burned
on one of the Royal Navy's blackest
days.

left
Maarten Harpertzoon Tromp was born
into a Dutch mercantile family in 1597.
A fine admiral, he fought many
engagements with the British,
particularly in the Second Dutch War.
He fell in action at Scheveningen in
1653.

action almost at will. It is a tribute
to the high morale of the Royal
Navy that the French accepted the
latter possibility not infrequently.

By the mid-eighteenth century
a combination of the Line-of-Battle
and outmatched ships was reducing almost every encounter to in-
decision and the official straitjacket
was loosened to give individual
designers some extra scope. The
average British warship was still
so obviously overgunned, however, that whenever the French
captured one, they immediately
reduced the armament if they

35

wished to use it themselves. In at least one engagement, the pursuit of a French squadron by a British one, resulted only in the capture of their slowest sailers – ex-British prizes! Fighting spirit and sheer numbers of ships compensated somewhat for weak design and we saw now the beginnings of the 'two-power standard', whereby the strength of the fleet was kept at a level sufficient to deal with any two fleets that could be brought against it. Thus, Britain could muster getting on for one third of Europe's warships, equal to the French and Dutch fleets combined. Spain was still fourth largest.

With its overall dominance established, the British fleet could now be used as a political instrument. A show of force was often enough to settle a point, but the art of carrying an army expeditionary force was developed together with their support whilst ashore. Operations were widespread, on the Peninsular and at Gibraltar, on Minorca and Sicily, in the West Indies and the Baltic; the navy developed a patient flexibility, an offshoot of which was the

right
Model of hull of the French first-rate *Soleil Royal* of 1669. French ships of this period were superior sailers to their British counterparts.

below
The captured *Royal Charles* being brought into Dutch waters. de Ruyter's raid on the Medway in 1667 had political repercussions in winning for the Netherlands better terms in the following peace treaty.

opposite, top
Longitudinally-sectioned French first-rate of 1693. Note particularly the complexities of the bowsprit at this time and its dependence upon the beakhead, not strictly part of the hull.

opposite, lower
Tromp. One of the best-known Dutch commanders, he had many successes against the British before falling at Scheveningen in 1653.

art of blockade. This slow strangle-hold it made its own, a form of warfare that could defeat even the most formidable of land powers.

In 1750, the fleet that carried out such a blockade had 126 ships of line status. These included four first rates, 10 second, 47 third (of a wide range of armament) and 65 fourth. These were supported by a further 80 fifth and six rates and a mixture of smaller craft, including sloops and cutters that were used much as despatch vessels and made ideal first commands producing

many seamen of high calibre. The small number of first rates will be noted. These were generally used as flag ships and were much larger than second rates, larger than the disparity in guns would convey, as they carried 42, 24 and 12-pounder weapons against the 32, 18 and 12-pounders of the 90-gunner. The 42-pounder was not a popular weapon, requiring a large gun crew, and it was gradually abandoned in favour of the handier 32.

Ammunition was varied. Besides the solid ball there was chain shot,

where the ball was split and connected by several links of chain. On firing, this whirled like a bolas, clearing rigging and personnel alike. A variation was barshot with sliding links replacing the chain. Canister shot was a collection of musket balls fired in a thin metal case or stout canvas bag, scattering on impact. Another variety was Langrage, which made use of any small metal scrap that came to hand instead of musket balls. The explosive shells fired from bomb ketches consisted of hollow iron balls filled with powder, and had a fuse that was ignited by the explosion of the propellent charge in the gun barrel. Solid and carcass shot could be heated and fired by ramming a wet wad between it and the firing charge; 'prematures' were common but their incendiary effect on the target was considerable. The solid ball was the most common projectile and, at 'half-pistol shot', could pierce a couple of feet of timber, reaching the inside of the ship in a deadly hail of splinters.

The standard British ship tactic was to work up to an adversary, holding fire completely until the whole broadside bore at virtually point-blank range, whereupon it was delivered simultaneously, usually leaving enemy gundecks a shambles and lower masts shot through. In the awful, shocked silence that followed, the British would quickly go about, if possible, to present their opposite broadside to stern galley. With no armoured transverse bulkheads to alleviate their effect, the second blow would slice through the enemy ship axially. The manoeuvre depended upon perfect timing and perfect discipline. Its effect was often deadly. The French much admired it but, except perhaps under Suffren, were never cool enough to practice it. All too often with the British, however, the rigid Line discipline stifled the possibilities of individual combat.

Maintenance and preservation on a wooden ship were considerable. In times of rapid fleet expansion, much inferior timber was used which rapidly 'went home' in more inaccessible places. Timber preparation was not well under-

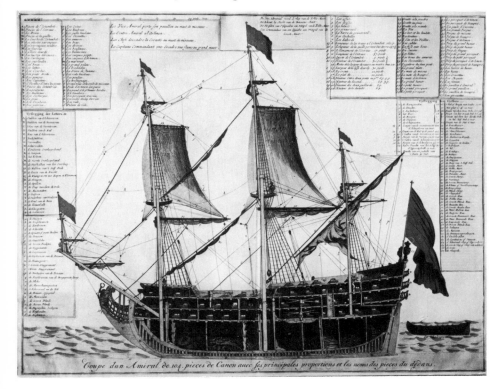

Coupe d'un Amiral de 104 pieces de Canon avec ses principales proportions et les noms des pieces du dedans.

stood. Initially it was 'charred', scorching one side whilst keeping the other wet. An improvement was 'stoving', where the timber was dried out by immersing it in wet sand, which was then heated. However, this was time consuming and gave way to steam drying and boiling.

External fouling was another problem, with marine growth on the hull soon having considerable effect on a ship's speed. A pitch-and-sulphur mix deterred growth and wood-boring creatures, a variation being reinforcement by stout paper or horsehair. These were only partially successful, the wood-boring being so serious that experiments were made in covering the whole ship's bottom with broad-head nails. This weighty and time-consuming process was superseded by one using a covering of lead sheets. As these were secured by iron nails they soon fell off due to galvanic action, and with copper sheets the same thing happened. Eventually copper sheets and copper nails were tried and found to be successful. Periods between dockings could thus be extended, an important factor in making full use of a fleet that had to spend ever more time at sea.

Conditions for the crew were being improved at this time with the importance of good diet and proper ventilation becoming appreciated.

Considering the vital need of accurate exchange of information between ships it is strange that so little attention had been paid it. Following a pre-action 'council-of-war' on the flagship, individual commanders were very much on their own. Sails were sometimes furled by design to convey a pre-agreed order or a flag hoisted where all could see it. Around 1770, Kempenfelt introduced a series of flaghoists which could be interpreted by reference to a signal book, but it was not until the nineteenth century that the introduction of Popham's system enabled a flag 'conversation' to be conducted.

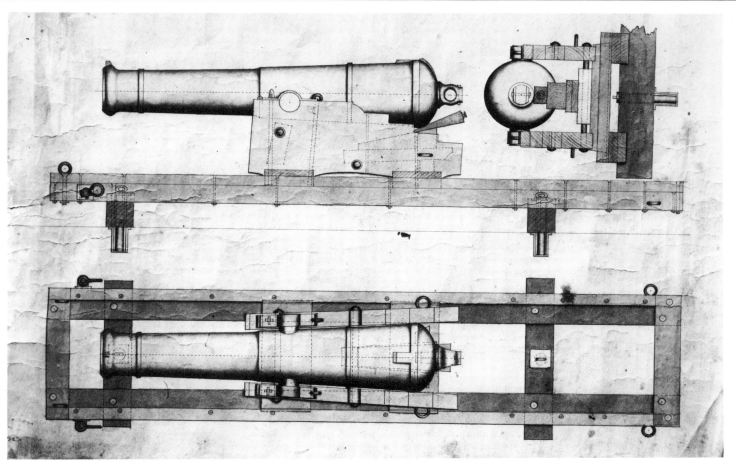

The Era of War

high noon of the sailing navy

Britain's Industrial Revolution brought the understanding of iron and with a new mastery of iron-founding, it soon replaced bronze for guns, being cheaper and also stronger. Improved casting and boring techniques resulted in consistently accurate bores, leaving smaller gaps, or 'windage' around a ball and enabling it to be fired further and more accurately on a smaller charge.

The premier foundry was that at Carron, which developed a short-barrelled gun for use on the company's own ships. It had thin sections for lightness and was mounted on a sliding carriage which permitted training and elevation as well as absorbing recoil. It was light enough to be handled by a gun crew of two and fired a very heavy ball over a short range. It so fitted with the Navy's ideas on attack that it immediately became popular under the name of Carronade. It could heft a 68-pound solid shot but was particularly deadly when loaded with grape, often double-shotted. It needed to be complemented by longer-ranged weapons but was used very effectively from the enemy's lee quarter, where his broadside could not bear but the heel of his ship laid bare his crowded upper deck. The resulting carnage is best described as 'marvellous unsavoury' (to quote from an earlier seaman's report on Grenville's *Revenge*) and the lee gauge of his tormentor prevented the victim's flight downwind.

Not only the French were causing headaches to Britain in the last quarter of the eighteenth century. The American colonies had opted for independence and to meet the needs of the inevitable war they had a few frigates, a large merchant fleet and plenty of determination. They followed earlier French tactics in preying on the British mercantile fleet and were aided by the Admiralty's seeming failure to grasp the gravity of the situation. Too few ships were allocated to the area but even these would have probably swung the balance but for the active intervention of the

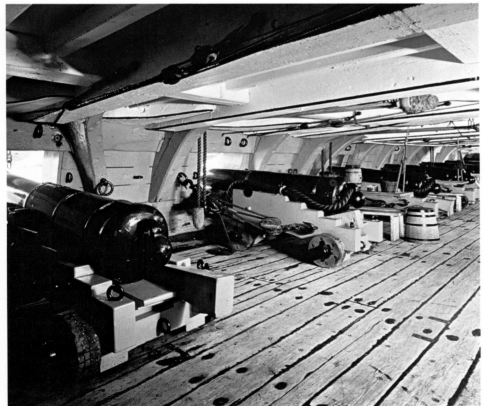

above
Trafalgar. The French *Redoutable* occupied the point in the line where Nelson chose to break through in *Victory*. Locked in combat with both *Victory* and *Temeraire*, the *Redoutable* eventually struck, but foundered the following day whilst under tow.

opposite
Battle of the Nile, 1798. The French fleet was anchored in a line in Aboukir Bay with their backs to shallow water and expecting an attack from seaward. Part of Nelson's force doubled round the head of the line and Bruey's force was destroyed from both sides.

left
32-pounders on one of the gundecks of H.M.S. *Victory*. The guns are run out and their implements housed under the low deckhead. Normally, at sea, the guns would be run in and their muzzles secured to the two eyebolts above the ports, which would be closed.

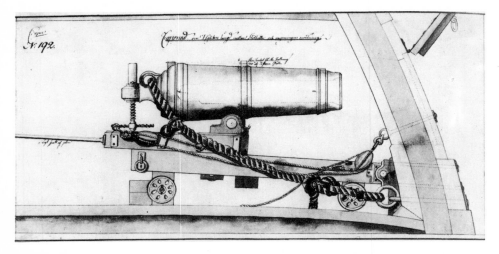

tality for actually getting beneath the anchored flagship *Eagle*, but he could not penetrate the ship's copper sheathing with the screw.

The British Navy, after a frustrating war, was greatly stimulated by Rodney's defeat of de Grasse at the Saintes in 1782. In this action the two fleets were evenly matched, but the British tactics deliberately broke the French line and defeated them mainly by superior gunnery. Their discipline was such that their rate of fire was often three times that of the French. Although victory was not pressed home as hard as it could have been, it was decisive and its lessons were not lost on one junior captain present. His name was Nelson. One prize taken was de Grasse himself, in his flagship *Ville de Paris*. This 104-gunner was larger than her British equivalents but

French, still smarting from the loss of Canada. Graves' indecisive action with de Grasse at the Chesapeake underlined the lack of understanding, but a far more prophetic event took place in the same waters in 1776, the world's first submarine attack.

The American love of innovation was typified by the *Turtle*. An appropriately named submersible of barrel shape, it was the brainchild of one Bushnell. The one-man crew propelled it vertically and horizontally by a pair of Archimedean screws, managing trim and ballast at the same time. Beneath his target the pilot was supposed to screw on an explosive charge. Sergeant Ezra Lee deserves immor-

found to be poorly constructed.

Britain was sorely pressed at this time, being at war with France, Spain and the Netherlands. The peace of 1783 was welcome to all and recognised the independence of the United States of America. However, just 10 years later war came once more through the ambitions of Napoleon. This called for the commissioning of reserve ships and new construction on a rapid time scale. Barham had rid the fleet support organisation of most of its graft and inefficiency, and ships joined the fleet at a rate never known before.

Ships were constructed and repaired in both Royal and private yards. The latter establishments were simple by today's standards, consisting largely of a slip and large baulks of timber on a tidal foreshore, usually close to a naturally wooded area. Buckler's Hard on Hampshire's Beaulieu River is a good example. Installations were minimal, consisting of sawpits, timber steaming facilities, carpenter's shops, smithies, capstans, sheerlegs and an endless succession of horse-drawn wagons with timber. When the local woods were finally exhausted, the slip was often taken up, the sheds demolished and the site left to return to its original state.

left
This model section of a wooden warship demonstrates its immense strength. The enormous number of grown timber knees is evident, together with the double planking of the hull. The stiffer, diagonal framing has not yet been introduced.

left, below
A gun's crew in action, 1800.

At the opening of this last war in a century of wars, the British fleet was 141 line ships strong, but only 12 were in commission. By early 1794 the number was 95, and Barham's great achievement here should not lightly be forgotten.

The Royal Navy immediately went on the offensive, its primary role being that of denying the sea to its enemy. Each French port harboured its contingent of ships, watched unceasingly by weather-beaten British squadrons, relieved in rota. The French, whose efficiency had not been improved by Revolutionary purges, declined in both morale and material through their inactivity. Their gaolers learned their trade the hard way, holding their stations relentlessly in fair weather and foul, close to a forbidding Biscay coast that allowed of no errors. Under cover of fog or bad weather French squadrons did break out from time-to-time but the greatest menace, as usual, came from privateers operating not only in the English Channel but as far afield as the Indian Ocean.

France had the land mass of Europe in its thrall and provoked a financial crisis in Britain, which had lost its main export markets. Even so, the slow pressure of blockade was having its effect with, valuable incoming French convoys also being taken, notably by Howe on the Glorious First of June in 1794. The Spaniards were soundly defeated by Jervis off St. Vincent in 1797 (ably assisted by Commodore Nelson) and it was the turn of the Dutch off Camperdown (Kampduin) in 1796. The Royal Navy had reached a pinnacle of superb, arrogant efficiency under a galaxy of fine commanders, Collingwood, Duncan, Jervis and

Howe; Hotham, Blackwood, Saumarez and Troubridge. Under them, the fleet rolled forward on the tide of its own success. Whether in hard-fought, ship-to-ship combat, as against the Revolutionnaire or the Droits de l'Homme or in returning the compliment of de Ruyter's Medway raid by taking 25 ships off Den Helder, it was unstoppable. But, among all the fine talent of its leaders, one stood out as a presiding genius. Nelson.

Napoleon's Egyptian adventure withered after his army watched Nelson destroy its supporting fleet at the Nile by tactics little short of unbelievable. Three years later at Copenhagen, in 1801, he destroyed the Danish fleet that was denying Britain's trade access to the Baltic. Loved by his men, he had a streak of absolute ruthlessness in action. His object was, simply, the annihilation of his enemy. Attack was pressed home as never before, weaknesses exploited and, if accepted doctrine was not the best for the occasion, it was ignored. Then, in 1805, Calder brought the combined Franco-Spanish fleet to bay, setting them up for interception by Nelson off Cape Trafalgar. The British fleet, outnumbered, divided and broke the enemy line into three. With no losses itself, it took 17 of the 33 enemy, but, in its greatest victory it suffered its greatest loss; its Admiral did not survive the action.

The fleet still had another 10 years of war before Napoleon was beaten, but it was never again

above
This impression of the Battle of Svenskund, fought in the Baltic in 1789, gives a good impression of contemporary manoeuvring and the smoke nuisance.

right, above
Nelson. A natural tactician; beloved by his men yet endowed with a ruthlessness that demanded nothing less than the total annihilation of his enemy.

right, centre
Howe. Victor at the Glorious First of June, 1794. Instrumental in the solution of the fleet mutinies of 1796 by obtaining redress for the legitimate grievances of the seamen.

right
John Jervis, Earl of St. Vincent, took his title from his great victory of 1797. As commander of the Channel Fleet he pursued the close blockade of the French ports.

seriously challenged. However, on the other side of the Atlantic, events were demonstrating that its success was due to morale and training rather than to superior warships.

The United States went to war with Britain in 1812. It was largely of Britain's making as she sought to reduce the American's share of seaborne trade. What particularly rankled among the Americans was the continued stopping of their ships for the impressment of any British subjects among the crew into His Majesty's service. The

fledgling U.S. Navy could boast no ships of the line but had developed the large frigate to the point where it could outgun any ship fast enough to catch it, and out-sail any ship that could out-gun it. Really the battle-cruiser before its time, this type of ship did not suffer from over-light scantlings, having construction equivalent to a British 74. There were only half a dozen of them, but they were commanded by first-rate seamen who had studied British methods. The Admiralty, at full stretch in Europe, could spare few ships for another apparent sideshow, but it was shocked into action as frigate after British frigate was worsted by these powerful giants. New traditions were created for the U.S.N., only slightly dented by Broke, whose *Shannon* managed to defeat the *Chesapeake*.

The Navy's immediate answer lay in the well-established concept of blockade and the Americans eventually found themselves as effectively corked in as the French had been. There were large British frigates in existence, the 60-gun *Leander* being an example, but they were very few and a stop-gap solution was to 'razee' three-deckers to two. These were never actually pitted in combat against the Americans but would certainly have been found wanting if they had been. They marked the beginning of a long line of large frigates which complemented the smaller 25 to 35-gun ships.

All this vast war-machine was about to be made obsolete, however, by a new force with which inventive men were tinkering.

left, above
The revenue cutter of 1803 shown here was not 'regular navy' but typifies the spirit of the many small armed craft which assisted the larger naval cruisers in the protection of English trade from the many French privateers over nearly a century of war.

left
The iron-bound Biscay coast allowed no error on the part of the close-blockading British squadrons. The *Magnificent* 74 wrecked outside Brest in 1804.

Steam

the new power at sea

The steam engine was no new panacea. Men had been trying, with varying degrees of success, to defeat the wind with steam for some 30 years. Symington's *Charlotte Dundas* showed the commercial possibilities, closely followed by the American Fulton's *Clermont* in 1807. It took the latter builder to produce the world's first mechanically powered warship after the outbreak of war in 1812. Named the *Demologos* she was really a catamaran frigate, with a single paddle wheel running, protected, between the hulls. She was armed with twenty-four 32-pounders and could have proved an embarrassment to the closely-investing British fleet had she been completed in time.

The sailing warship did not vanish all at once but embarked on its final phase at the beginning of the century of peace that followed the defeat of Napoleon. That happy event had found the Royal Navy with over 900 listed ships, of which the 'liners' were dominated by almost 80 of the ubiquitous 74's. Wholesale scrapping followed, but the two-power capability was retained, notably over a powerful Russian navy and a French fleet that was again a sizable force.

It may seem at first sight strange that an industrially supreme country such as Britain should not rapidly adopt steam power. But we see here the first of those apparent paradoxes in the Admiralty, which seemed reluctant to exploit a new development. The truth was, of course, that the Royal Navy was so dominant that there was little point in making it obsolete overnight. What was important was that any

important development abroad could still be countered on an overwhelming scale. Although not immediately apparent, improvements were still being made to sailing ships. Many of these were the work of Seppings, a famous Surveyor of the Navy, who re-introduced diagonal reinforcement of ships frames, giving extra stiffness to resist hogging and enabling lengths to be increased.

Further improvements were made at bow and stern. Forecastles had been little more than a flimsy 'beak' built on to the hull

Fulton's steamer *Clermont* of 1807 was not designed for military purposes, but her obvious potential in steaming upstream from New York to Albany enabled her designer to get backing for the steam frigate *Demologos*.

proper and giving little protection against raking fire from ahead. Seppings, and his successor Symonds, extended the hull framing up through the forecastle and topped it off with a high, stout bulwark.

An even more attractive target

was offered by the enormous expanse of glass in the squared-off stern galleries, supported on a weak and vulnerable transom. Even with the new round and elliptical sterns much glass remained, but a stout transverse bulkhead was added to prevent the gundecks getting the full effect of a raking broadside from astern. The new bow and stern configurations also allowed more guns to be sited to fire along the ship's axis and quarters. The high, protective bulwark forward was then continued aft along either side of the weatherdeck. It was high enough to require a walkway along the top, conveniently joining forecastle to poop. This walkway rapidly widened until it formed a continuous light spar deck, covering the waist and supporting spare spars and boats.

About 1830 composite construction was introduced as timber became more difficult to obtain. The first metal components to be introduced were iron knees, joining deck beams to side frames and not easy to make from wood in the quantities required.

The rating of warships, never straightforward, was further complicated after the Napoleonic Wars by being re-defined as follows: First rates, over 100 guns; Second, 80–100; Third, 70–80; Fourth, 50–70; Fifth, 36–50; and Sixth, 24–36. With improved construction, ships could be built larger and the last of the sailing, three-decked, first-rates such as the French *Valmy* could boast of 120 guns. The big sailing frigates, which had so impressed the British Admiralty in the 1812 war, were being built as 50-gunners into the Victorian era although out-done by the larger French 60's.

It was decided about this time to standardise on the 32-pounder in British ships where possible to simplify logistics. Those that had to be mounted high were made shorter in the barrel for lightness, improving neither accuracy nor range.

The French fleet, although large, was small by British standards and would have welcomed a development to render its large neighbour obsolete. As in Britain, steam-power was being investigated in France, but no great break-through seemed imminent. Far more promising was the explosive shell, the effect of which on wooden ships was being loudly championed by Paixhans. This idea, again, was not new. Bomb ketches had lobbed them for years but, when fired in low trajectory, their ballistic properties were peculiar as, after being filled with explosive, the sphere's centre of gravity was rarely in the centre. They were also a great fire hazard and it is possible that the destruction of the French flagship *l'Orient* at the Nile was due to an accident with a French shell.

This new Gallic enthusiasm for the shell was taken seriously by the British, who established a base for gunnery experiment on Collingwood's old flagship *Excellent* in Portsmouth Harbour. If any doubts still existed about the effectiveness of the explosive shell, they were dispelled at Sinope in 1853, when a Russian squadron armed with Paixhan guns blew apart an inferior Turkish force. This is to anticipate, however, for with the Victorian era began an age where invention

was king and developments came rapidly.

Unarmed, steam-propelled despatch vessels had been in service with the Royal Navy since the 1820's, but the first true steam warship was the wooden paddle-sloop *Gorgon*, with a low-power direct-acting engine. The Admiralty introduced it in answer to the French, who were moving in the direction of steam. The paddle was an embarrassment to a warship as it interfered with its sailing qualities (it should be remembered that the steam engine was still only an auxiliary to sail) and it was vulnerable to damage from weather and the enemy. Thus the marine screw with its deep immersion saw intensive development on both sides of the Atlantic. The American *Princeton* had the distinction of being the world's first screw-propelled warship; the engineer concerned was Ericsson, later famous for his *Monitor*.

By the 1840's, Britain was cutting frigates in two halves and adding a new centre section, complete with engine; these were rapidly followed by large, purpose-built ships which were equipped with lifting propellers. To reduce drag, these could be hoisted into a trunk forward of the rudder post when not in use. Funnels were made telescopic and housed when sailing and the order 'Up funnel, down screw,' became a by-word.

The Royal Navy's first screw-propelled warship was the sloop *Rattler* and, to settle the controversy as to whether the screw was superior to the paddle, a

slightly unscientific tug-of-war with the paddle-driven *Alecto* was staged in 1845. Satisfied on the screw's potential, the Admiralty soon commissioned the 60-gun *Ajax* and 90-gun *Agamemnon* as the first 'liners' so equipped.

Also about this time gunnery tests were made on the small and rather rusty *Ruby* to establish whether iron warships would be more resistant to shell fire than wooden. In spite of reservations, the 1850-ton *Trident* was ordered, to become the Navy's first iron warship.

With the increasing lethal effect of marine guns, experiments were now being conducted with various combinations of wood, iron and proprietary compounds to give maximum protection. During the Crimean War, Britain and France were allies and a combined fleet was repulsed by the forts at Sebas-

topol. The French answer lay in five, cumbersome floating batteries, roofed-in and covered with heavy plate. They survived close under the guns of Kinburn and reduced it. Armour plate had arrived.

On the Baltic front of the same war, Captain Cowper Coles mounted a 68-pounder on a turntable and installed it on a raft for inshore counter-battery work. It inspired his later work on turrets. The Russians, resenting all this enemy naval activity on their doorstep, produced floating explosive mines detonated by the now familiar technique of an acid-filled contact horn.

In the midst of all these advances, it is worth recording that 1854 saw what was probably the last fight by rowed warships when the Russian Kanonjollars engaged a British force in the Baltic. These 25-metre craft,

49

above
1842 saw the first wooden frigate rebuilt to take steam paddle propulsion, followed within four years by the first purpose-built screw frigate. Almost within a decade this, too, was outmoded by the iron single-decker. Shown here is the wooden U.S.S. *Lancaster* of 1858.

opposite, top
Dupuy de Lôme's ironclad *Gloire* of 1858 was inspired largely by the success of the ironclad floating wooden batteries used in the Crimea. The weight of armour restricted her to only one gun deck, as in her rivals, so that they became known, misleadingly, as frigates.

opposite, lower
Topmasts sent down, the *St George* 120 and *James Watt* 91 ride an unlikely Baltic sea during the Royal Navy's operations on the other front of the 'Crimea' War.

right, lower
The American 'side-wheeler' *Mississippi* was one of a pair of 1,700-tonners dating from 1841. During an eventful career she was a unit of Perry's Japan Expedition and took part in both the Mexican War and operations during the Civil War on the river that shared her name.

above, right
A Civil War picture of the crew of the historic American ironclad *Monitor*. The massive single turret here has the gun run in and is rigged with an awning to reduce the almost intolerable temperature within.

with 10 pairs of oars, mounted a 24-pounder at either end and were directly descended from the galleys, a pedigree of some 2,500 years. In the skerries and archipelagoes of the Baltic the various forms of rowed warship had survived purely because of their manoeuvrability. The redoubtable Henrik af Chapman created a variety of such craft for use against Russia, and similar Danish ships proved a menace against the large British convoys entering the Baltic during the Napoleonic Wars.

The Crimean War defined the essential ingredients for the next generation of warships – steam propulsion, shell-firing guns and armour protection.

Distinction should be made between iron construction and armour protection. The French Crimea floating batteries (and later British copies) were wooden-built, covered with iron plates. The *Ruby* experiments had shown that the iron of the day was too inconsistent in quality to be fully relied upon to resist shell-fire, and thus the first iron frigate then building, the *Birkenhead*, was remodelled as a troop-transport. Her famous wreck, off South Africa in 1852, was not attributable to her iron construction. She filled rapidly due to the large apertures that had been cut in her bulkheads during her conversion.

Although the Admiralty had written-off iron construction for the moment, they still fully appreciated the value of armoured protection. They knew that two of the French gunboats at Kinburn had suffered a total of 135 hits, virtually without casualty. Typically, no overt move was made to produce a design which would have caused large-scale obsolescence within the Royal Navy and there matters would probably have rested but for the French designer Dupuy de Lôme. In his *Gloire* of 1858 he

produced a trump card to challenge his rivals. She was an uncompleted wooden two-decker, razed to a single tier and protected by four-inch iron plates secured externally above the waterline. She introduced a new low look, for armour could not be used to cover the whole expanse of a multi-decker's sides. Her machinery was powerful enough to give over 13 knots and confidence in it was sufficient to build her without a sailing rig, although a full three-mast rig was later added. By contrast, in those days of thirsty and inefficient engines, British ships retained their sailing rigs for many years to guarantee the required cruising range. However, with her 36 breech loading guns firing 66-pound shells, the French saw the *Gloire* as the immediate counter to the all-wood ship-of-the-line and immediately ordered more.

Before the *Gloire* was even in the water, however, the British laid down their own challenge, the famous *Warrior*. Launched in 1860, she showed conclusively that the recent prejudice against iron con-

struction had been overcome. By framing her in iron, she was given the strength to support protection and sub-division on a scale impossible in the wooden-framed Frenchman. Only the length of the central battery was protected, including enclosing transverse bulkheads. Either end, including steering gear, was left unprotected. Her horizontal trunk engines of 5,500 hp gave her about $14\frac{1}{2}$ knots and she carried 68-pounder guns. She was advanced but only slightly ahead of the French *Couronne* which was built of iron, had a second tier of guns and re-introduced the ram.

Both navies were now in a race which, with other eventual contenders, was to last for over 60 years. Design was now crucial, for the three principal parameters defining a warship had become clear – speed, armament and protection. Any one could be improved only at the expense of the others and designers had to take advantage of every technological advance.

From 1861, the American Civil War stimulated further innovation.

H.M.S. AGINCOURT,
IRON-CLAD 28 GUNS.
Flag Ship of the Western Division of the Channel Squadron.
Published by H.M Currie. 79. Union St. Stonehouse Devon.

The Confederates constructed a self-propelled armoured battery called the *Merrimac*. Although little advance on the French Crimea gunboats, she posed a threat that was met by Ericsson's famous *Monitor*. This was a low freeboard, iron-and-teak raft 172 feet in length overlaying a conventional hull 124 feet long. There was no superstructure beyond funnels and hatches and Ericsson's masterpiece, a single, massive rotating turret, containing two 11-inch muzzle-loaders. Their eventual inconclusive encounter is not important compared with the principle established. Designers such as Ericsson and Cowper Coles were writing the obituary for the broad-side battery ship.

Other interesting craft of the Civil War were the so-called 'Davids'. These steam-propelled craft could be trimmed down by ballasting to offer the smallest possible target. They were then supposed to ram a spar torpedo – a charge on a long pole – into a target's side. Their one victim, the *Housatonic*, not surprisingly took her attacker up with her in the explosion but another step had been taken in the eventual development of the submarine.

The beginning of the decade had seen the introduction of the iron warship and the end saw the last of the wooden ships-of-the-line pay off. Progress indeed.

right
Much of a fleet's work is involved in inshore support, a function often eclipsed by the set-piece battle. Here, in a typical incident, the steam paddle sloop *Vesuvius* supports gunboats in reduction of installations on the Bielosarrai Spit during the Crimean War.

below
The *Couronne* was the first all-iron line warship to be laid down. She was launched in 1860, but the French were four months behind the British *Warrior*, which took the honours.

Transition
the end of the sailing navy

Whilst all these major events tend to take the attention, it should not be forgotten that the great Imperial Powers, particularly Britain, continued to police their empires with a large number of auxiliary sloops, corvettes and gunboats, some of wood and some of composite construction. In those pre-radio days their masters were men of many parts, acting often on their own initiative, sometimes succouring the distressed, sometimes smiting the wrongdoer. Truly formidable men, their ships lasted a further 30 years before being superseded by the more versatile third-class cruisers.

The arrival of the turret, meanwhile, did not mean the overnight disappearance of the central-battery ship. The increasing size of guns meant that fewer could be carried, but utilisation was maximised by their being mounted on carriages running on traversing slides to enable them to cover either beam. To enable the heavy armour to be made as thick as possible the guns were closely grouped amidships, typified in the *Bellerophon* of 1865, and the sides ahead and abaft the battery given marked tumble-home – excessive in some French designs – to improve firing arcs. Some were protected from axial fire by heavy transverse bulkheads. These were termed 'box battery' ships.

As already noted, de Lôme included rams on his iron ships. These were possible of course only when there was no sailing rig to demand a bowsprit. Several European navies included them as an inexpensive weapon and they gained credance at the Battle of Lissa in

The American broadside ironclad *New Ironsides* was built in 1861 and accidentally destroyed by fire in 1866 after an active career in the Union fleet during the Civil War. In the campaign against Charleston she was put out of action for a year after a 'David' had exploded a spar torpedo against her quarter.

top
The Victorian coast-defence monitor H.M.S. *Glatton* was built in 1871 as one of a series of ironclad rams. Their sudden popularity was a result of the Battle of Lissa in 1866, but their 12-knot speed and low endurance rendered them next to useless. The turret contained two 12-inch muzzle-loaders.

right
The single-screw corvette *Tenedos* had a
barque rig and was typical of the smaller
cruising ships of the Victorian Navy.
Her career was only 1870–87 as the type
was displaced by the third-class
protected cruisers which were equipped
with reliable machinery.

below
The Royal Navy's large iron frigates of
the 1870's sacrificed protection for
armament and speed, and were built
largely because of the success of similar
American ships of the Civil War. H.M.S.
Shah engaged the renegade Peruvian
armoured turret ship *Huascar* in an
inconclusive action in 1876.

1866, where the Italian flagship, stationary at the time, was lost to the Austro-Hungarians by ramming. The fact that the purpose-built Italian turret ram *Affondatore* was present and failed dismally to contact any moving target did not deter foreign 'experts' from hailing the new weapon and uselessly equipping warships with it for the next 40 years.

The short-lived turret ram was designed to keep her target under fire whilst she advanced, end-on, to deliver a *coup-de-grâce* by the ram. They were not popular with the British who insisted on the retention of rigging. As this, of course, obstructed firing arcs a peculiar type evolved in the *Monarch* of 1868. She was a compromise with two turrets, each housing twin 12-inch muzzle-loaders, sited amidships and buried under a spardeck supporting full rigging. Although

the firing arcs were inevitably restricted, the few guns still commanded greater zones than on broadside ships and less weight of armour was required. She was, however, crank and with poor accommodation. *The Captain*, incorporating Cowper Coles ideas, was commissioned shortly afterwards. Standing rigging was reduced by the use of tripod masts and the turrets were sited at gun-deck level between forecastle and poop structures. Her celebrated foundering resulted in a brief return to the central battery ship.

The turret ram, related to the *Monitor* and refined through various coast defence craft (known as 'breastwork monitors'), was the direct inspiration for the *Devastation*, which finally ended the Royal Navy's adherence to the sailing rig. She again carried two turrets but on a low freeboard hull and separated by a simple super-structure.

below, centre
Gun drill aboard the *Minotaur* of 1868, probably taken in the 1870's. A 9-inch muzzle-loading rifle is on the right-hand side of the picture, on a traversing carriage. The forest of rigging of the five masts gives some idea of the difficulties facing those who wished to incorporate rotating gun turrets into warships.

below
The 12-inch muzzle-loader of the British ironclad ram *Hotspur* of 1870. The turret was fixed, with the single gun revolving within it on a turntable and run out for firing through any one of four embrasures.

bottom
This study of Cowper Coles' turret-ship *Captain* of 1869 shows clearly the turret disposition beneath the light 'flying-deck' joining forecastle to poop. Note how the tripod masts have reduced the quantity of standing rigging.

Odd derivatives were the so-
called Popoffkas, built for the
Russian Navy for inshore use.
They were circular in plan. In
theory, this gave a very stable gun
platform but in practice they
proved virtually unmanageable.

With reliance now placed on
fewer guns it is readily apparent
that these must have been greatly
improved. Up to the mid-nine-
teenth century, the cannon on its
carriage had changed little over
300 years, although more reliable
powder and more accurate bores
were steadily increasing both
accuracy and range. Improved techniques included the first sights and
calibration made possible through
adjustable mountings, which in
turn permitted training and elevation, and absorbed recoil without
a mass of breechings. The slow
match and gunlock gave way to
the instantaneous percussion tube.

To stabilise the shell in flight it was given spin by shaping helically or rifling the gun's bore, which meant that the projectile had to be ballistically shaped rather than spherical. These proved difficult to load via the muzzle and so the breech-loader was re-introduced. Early breeches were difficult to make gas-tight, and so many accidents occurred through premature firings with the breech improperly secured that the British reverted to the slow-firing muzzle-loader. Both the American and German navies developed effective breech-locking devices so that, until the 1880's when the Royal Navy again adopted breech-loading, foreign practice was well ahead.

Armstrong's developed a barrel of concentric shrunk-on sleeves which, married to the American-pattern of interrupted-screw breech mechanism, proved to be out-standingly accurate and reliable. Muzzle-loaders needed to be short in the barrel – and thus inaccurate – in order to run them back into the turret for re-loading. Breech-loaders suffered no such restrictions and were made much longer. Being stronger than cast guns, the new designs could accept larger charges and the result was a higher muzzle-velocity, greater range, accuracy, repeatability and – more significantly – greater penetrative power. A new competition developed between gun and armour manufacturers.

These revolutions tended, of course, to be concentrated on capital ships, where their effect would be greatest. But Britain also had a large force of imperial cruisers, though nothing to match the threat typified by the fast and heavily armed American *Wampanoag*, representative of a force of fast commerce raiders used with great effect during the Civil War. These were answered by the large, unarmoured iron frigate, fast under sail or power. They were box battery ships with a bewildering variety of guns in their armament, not only 9 and 7-inch but sometimes 6-inch as well.

The *Shah* of this type fought the famous duel in 1877 with the Peruvian turret-ship *Huascar*, crewed by revolutionaries. The result of the action was predictable, with the faster *Shah* hitting her target almost at will but failing to pierce her armour, due to the low muzzle velocity of the projectiles. The slow *Huascar* was unable to use her ram and eventually escaped inshore. One notable incident was the launching by the *Shah* of a Whitehead torpedo, which missed. This weapon was not used successfully until the following year when

below
Calliope was among the last of the Royal
Navy's sailing corvettes, dating from
1884. Their metal hulls were sheathed
with wood and their four 6-inch guns
were sited on sponsons. The 4,000 hp of
her compound engines were just
sufficient to enable the *Calliope* to survive
the Samoa hurricane which wrecked the
American and German ships present.

right, centre
The 'Admirals' of 1884–86 were good
examples of barbette ships, with their
faired 13.5-inch breechloaders mounted
very high. The *Howe* is shown here
about the turn of the century, shortly
before the Victorian livery was
abandoned.

right
Four 16-inch, 80-ton muzzle-loaders
were carried in two turrets mounted en
echelon amidships in H.M.S. *Inflexible*
of 1876. Only the amidships citadel was
armoured. Other novel features were
passive stabilizer tanks and the carrying
of two 60-foot torpedo boats.

opposite, top
Originally designed to be brig-rigged,
H.M.S. *Warspite* and her sister
Imperieuse dated from 1881 and became
the navy's first armoured mastless
cruisers. Their marked tumble-home and
wing turrets were decidedly Gallic in
flavour. They served long as Pacific
flagships and *Warspite* is here seen
leaving Panama.

below
The armour and ram of H.M.S.
Dreadnought of 1875, built as an improved
Devastation. Note also that the forward
turret is trained to starboard with the
12.5-inch 38-ton, muzzle-loaders run in.
The stocked anchors and their catting
davits are also prominent.

a Russian warship sank a Turkish
auxiliary.

The term 'torpedo' had
previously referred to a mine but
the new development, known as
the 'locomotive torpedo', was proposed as a wire-guided explosive
craft, controlled remotely to
explode against a target. The idea
was that of an Austrian named
Luppis and was rejected as imprac-
ticable. His cooperation with
Whitehead refined it to a cigar-
shaped submersible, propelled by
compressed air. It contained most
of the major components of its
modern counterpart and was an
immediate success, with no navy
feeling that it could ignore it.

The new weapon indeed posed a
considerable threat when carried
by a small but fast ship, with the

French being early in the field in
1876. Their craft was very frail and
the Thornycroft boat *Lightning* of
the following year was larger and
more seaworthy. Torpedo boats
rapidly became a sales success to
all navies with slender means, for
they had the appeal of a potentially
lethal punch for a very small outlay. Thornycroft, Yarrow and
White became names synonymous
with a long succession of these slim
craft, which contained little but
machinery, had almost non-existent
accommodation and were of restricted sea-going capacity. The
British Admiralty, typically, did
not rush into building great numbers but commenced work on a
counter-measure.

With increasing power available
from boilers of higher pressure and
compound machinery, some schools
of thought favoured the mounting
of the heaviest armament on a light
hull, relying on speed for protection.
This idea made sense to the
Italian navy, interested only in the
short distances in the Mediterranean where large bunker and
stores capacity was unnecessary
and speed was very useful. Thus
the two Duilio class of 1876
mounted two twin 17.7-inch gun
turrets – the largest that
Armstrongs could build. These
were sited in echelon for the
greatest field of fire and were
muzzle-loading, although their
length prohibited their being with-
drawn into their turrets. The
barrels could be depressed and
shells rammed home from an
armoured glacis on the adjacent
deck. Armour was up to 22-inches
in thickness and, understandably,
was limited only to a central citadel,
enclosing magazines, machinery
and the barbettes on which the
turrets rotated.

Britain, predictably, produced a
counter in the 11,900-ton *Inflexible*
with 16-inch guns. Anachronistic-
ally, she was for a time rigged as a
brig. Ships of this type were rather
unsuccessful, but later units
reduced the main calibre to 12-inch
in order to re-introduce the breech-
loader. The rate of fire per barrel
was only about two rounds per
minute as the turret needed to be
aligned with apertures in the

adjacent superstructure to accept each projectile.

French designs then inspired a reversal to the more practical layout of the *Devastation* of a decade earlier. The drawback was the larger area that needed to be protected and, thus, the weight. The solution was thoroughly unsatisfactory, with the abandonment of the heavy turret and the mounting of large breech loaders on the open, revolving top of the barbettes. The vulnerability of the gun crew and hazards of loading under fire need no elaboration. All the class were named after Admirals and the last, *Benbow*, boasted a pair of 16.25-inch guns. Speed was supposed to be the strongpoint of the class but their freeboard was so low that in any sea at all they were awash at well below their 17-knot maximum. Other navies experimented briefly with barbette ships, but soon abandoned the idea.

The next British pair, in 1887, were larger in order to accommodate improvements, and featured a low forecastle and an afterdeck one level higher. They included the ill-fated *Victoria*, destined to be

right
In answer to the Italian *Duilio*'s 17.7-inch guns, H.M.S. *Inflexible* of 1876 carried muzzle-loading 16-inch in echeloned turrets. She is shown here as originally rigged as a brig, although this tophamper was soon removed.

below
The sinking of H.M.S. *Victoria* by the *Camperdown* off the Syrian coast in 1893 was not only a first magnitude disaster; it also provided 'ammunition' for the protagonists of the ram.

opposite, top
H.M.S. *Undaunted* of 1886 was a belted cruiser which carried her mixed 9.2 and 6-inch armament at a useful height. Although well protected, the type suffered from having a too-low margin of speed superiority over the battleships that they were supposed to track.

opposite, lower
The armoured gunboat *Cockatrice* of 1886 was typical of the small, rigged cruising ships that maintained the presence of the Victorian navy around the world.

sunk in collision with the *Camper-down* in 1893. She again featured the ponderous 16.25's with their slow rate of fire, but these were afterwards abandoned for smaller weapons with improved performance. *Victoria*'s other feature was the first triple-expansion engine in a British battleship.

All these developments were made against a background of increasing Franco-Russian friendship and the sum of their combined naval strengths was the potential threat against which the Royal Navy built. Other fleets, particularly those of American and Japan, were growing, but were looked upon as 'friendly', not particularly innovatory, and outside British spheres of interest. A newly unified Germany was beginning enviously to look at British power through colonial strength, and commenced the build-up of a fleet as a means of acquiring an empire for itself.

More specifically, the Admiralty took the threat of the torpedo very seriously. Torpedo-boats were now operated by many fleets and the French, disappointed at the impotence of its fleet during its defeat in the Franco-Prussian War, had slowed down major construction in favour of first-class torpedo-boats. Answers to the threat included a tertiary battery of quick-firing guns and torpedo nets to hang around ships when at anchor. Encouragement was given also to improved speed and manoeuvrability.

It has already been noted that the early protected iron ships had only one gundeck and because of this they were known either as frigates or corvettes. These were patently misnomers for such powerful vessels and the term 'Masted Cruiser' became current. With improvements in machinery, the sailing rigs were abandoned with the *Warspite* of 1883, and the name 'Cruiser' was adopted. Their duties were mainly imperial policing and acting as 'eyes' to the main fleet. With four 9.2-inch guns in single mountings, *Warspite* was really a scaled-down battleship.

Sail persisted for a while as an auxiliary in smaller cruisers and among the last ships so equipped

was the *Calliope*, whose escape from Apia during the Samoa hurricane made world headlines. Soon afterwards, however, the first of a new breed of fast, elegant cruisers appeared from the Elswick yard of Vickers. Their influence on contemporary design was profound and many were long-lived.

Rapid development of the U.S. Navy about this time provoked much agitation in the British press to the effect that the 'two-power standard' was a thing of the past. Extra patriotic stimulus was provided by the Golden Jubilee Review of 1887 and the result was the Naval Defence Act of 1889. The main fruits of this were the Royal Sovereigns. With longer hulls and greater freeboard they

could maintain their speed in a seaway and weight was saved by the adoption of steel armour. Nevertheless, the four 13.5-inch guns were still in open-topped barbettes. These guns had the advantage of new cast-steel armour-piercing shells, which could penetrate the thickest known armour without breaking up, and there were firing charges of cordite, a new slow-burning propellent vastly superior to the old powder charges and making far less smoke. Its performance was more consistently predictable and it generated higher muzzle velocity.

The last of the class was the *Hood*, modified to incorporate proper turrets. The modern battleship had arrived.

Naval Rivalries

the race to war

The Naval Defence Act was an action typical of a major power whose might rested on absolute supremacy at sea and which realised that it could lose it. Major European navies could now number their torpedo boats in hundreds. Although untried in action and something of a bogey, they presented an undeniable threat. This was to be countered by the Torpedo Boat Destroyer, later simply 'Destroyer', a larger craft more capable of maintaining her speed and carrying a smaller number of torpedoes to give space for a 12-pounder and three 6-pounder guns. Yarrow's *Havock* of 1892 was the first of a series known as the '27-knotters' and the beginning of the most glamorous type of ship yet evolved.

For attack purposes, the Royal Navy introduced the torpedo gun-boat, typified by the elegant little *Halcyons*, but these were a failure through a lack of speed sufficient to deliver an attack without getting severely mauled in the process. The quick-firing, or Q.F., gun was evolved to enable capital ships to stop torpedo-boats outside their launching range. Their high rate of fire was made possible by the introduction of the cartridge case, which combined projectile and firing charge. The earlier short-ranged weapons, such as the multi-barrelled Gatling, Hotchkiss and Nordenfeldt became obsolete.

As the early armoured cruisers of the main navies were too ponderous to be of a much practical use, a new type of 'protected cruiser' emerged with armour on a lighter scale. Their high speed made them potentially useful as

commerce raiders, a threat the British took most seriously. Typical were the American *Baltimores*, but more obviously a menace were the French 23-knot *Chateaurenaults*. The main fault of the type was the tendency to too large a calibre in main armament, resulting in a slow rate of fire, but the threat was compounded by the Russian *Rurik* and the French *Dupuy de Lôme* of 1890, the exaggerated ram bow and tumblehome of which typify the French warship of the time.

The British answer lay in the two *Powerfuls*, four-funnelled monsters of over 14,000 tons, designed to run down any raider. Their new, high-pressure water-tube boilers powered them for an easy 22 knots and they were 520 feet in length. More imposing than battleships, they were not protected, their 9.2-inch guns being designed to keep a fight at a distance. It was note-worthy in this respect that *Terrible* was commanded by Percy Scott, a

above
H.M. Torpedo Boat No. 42 in 1889. These little craft varied greatly in size and appearance, with torpedoes launched either from tubes or davits. The largest were of only 130 tons and their limitations in a seaway encouraged the development of the larger TBD.

opposite, top
The transitional state of the warship in 1891 is well shown in this visit of a French squadron to the Russians at Kronstadt. The leading French unit is the battleship *Marengo*, designed by Dupuy de Lôme and launched in 1869.

opposite, lower
The blowing-up of the American armoured cruiser *Maine* in 1898 at Havana was a prime factor in the commencement of the Spanish-American War. The true cause, however, was almost certainly unstable cordite, rather than sabotage, a source of destruction of many other warships.

top
Torpedo Boat No. 75 in 1891. The appearance of these craft differed considerably, depending upon the building yard. They typically mounted two torpedo tubes aft and a third firing through the stem. The 14-inch Woolwich torpedo had a range of 1,000 yards at 15½ knots and carried a 33-lb gun-cotton warhead.

above
This 1894 picture of the '27-knotter' A-class TBD *Contest* on her trials gives an idea of the amount of hull space devoted to her triple expansion engines. The 42 A-class boats were the Royal Navy's first TBDs and carried a 12-pounder gun and two 18-inch torpedo tubes.

specialist who, with the American, Bradley Fiske, brought gunnery to the state of a science, introducing new drills to take advantage of optical sights and range finders.

The Powerfuls in turn brought answers from abroad, the Italian Garibaldis, the French Jeanne d'Arcs and the German *Fürst Bismarck* being typical. Their common features were a powerful main battery in two turrets, one forward and one aft, and a casemated secondary armament along the sides.

About the turn of the twentieth century, to counter foreign construction, the Royal Navy reverted briefly to the armoured cruiser, with its more powerful main battery, but once again they could not be counted successful, though

probably the best examples were the pair of German Scharnhorsts of 1906.

The phenomenal growth of the German fleet since the appointment of Tirpitz in 1897 was a matter of great concern to the British. With an almost evangelical zeal he set out to build a fleet to spread 'Germanism' in an Anglo-Saxon dominated world. Collision was inevitable.

Battleships took the water, class by class. After the Royal Sovereigns came the Majestics, retaining the athwartships funnels but introducing the 12-inch gun; then the Canopus, Formidable and Duncan classes with the same standard layout and conventionally sited funnels. With the last class at the turn of the century, the old Victorian livery of black hulls, white upperworks and buff funnels, gave way to standard grey 'crabfat', as if to underline a new businesslike approach to the foreign threat.

The German fleet was by now, far too large for purely defensive purposes and British public opinion demanded 'we want eight'. The result was the King Edward VII's (known to the Fleet as the 'Wobbly Eight' because of their eccentric

敵旗艦自爆水雷沈没マコロフ夫提督以下乗員八百共魚腹

帝國艦隊旅順攻撃

top
A Japanese version of an incident aboard the Russian flagship *Petropavlovsk* during the fleets' indecisive encounter in February 1904, the year before Tsushima.

above
The February 1904 encounter between the Russian and Japanese was indecisive largely because of rigid adherence to the line of battle, in spite of ranges dropping to below 8,000 yards. Here Togo's line is led by his flagship *Mikasa*, the nearest ship being *Shikishima*.

station-keeping habits) and even the purchase of a pair of battleships building for Chile.

One aspect of German design was the adoption of lighter calibre main armament than the British, e.g. 11-inch against 12-inch and 8.2-inch against 9.2-inch. The weight saved was used to improve protection and sub-division.

In spite of its size – or because of it – the Royal Navy of the late Victorian years had developed without action experience. Thus, every skirmish of every war, however small, was scrutinised for 'lessons'. The 1894 Yalu River action appeared to prove that lightly-armoured but fast ships with many Q.F. guns could outfight more heavily armed ships with slow rates of fire. In practice, the Chinese were beaten by the spirit

of the Japanese attack, with a fleet trained in British techniques. And the crushing of a Spanish force off Manila in 1898 was by an American force so superior that it proved nothing. Thus the great race into the twentieth century was one of applications of technologies yet untried.

Some answers were given when Russia and Japan went to war in 1904. The Japanese opened with a surprise torpedo attack by destroyers on the Russian fleet anchored outside Port Arthur. Success was limited even against this 'soft' target; the bogey of the mass destroyer attack was partially laid.

The hard pressed Russian Pacific Fleet was to be reinforced by the Baltic Fleet, which sailed halfway around the world, only to be intercepted by Togo in the Tsushima

Strait. After months of slow steaming the Russian morale was as poor as the condition of their ships. The faster Japanese cruisers used their speed and disciplined gunnery constantly to smother the ponderous Russian battleships. The latter's armour saved them from mortal injury but they were herded and tormented on to the waiting iron ring of Togo's heavy ships and were devastated. Speed and perfect order had won the day and the 12-inch gun was queen of the seas.

As the multiplicity of cannon had been rationalised to improve the logistics of the sailing navy, so this exercise was again required with the wide variety of calibres of the new navy. When all were firing together, it was difficult to spot and correct for individual guns. The big-gun advocates pointed out

below
Although completed only five years before *Dreadnought*, the Russian battleship *Tsarevitch*'s appearance emphasises the radical design of the former ship. The Russian ship was built in France and features the pronounced tumble-home so characteristic of their designs.

opposite, centre
A Canopus-class battleship with her anti-torpedo nets rigged whilst at anchor during the First World War. Note the supplementary floats carried right aft, in addition to the ship's normal large boat complement.

that to realise their advantages,
deliberate shooting from the maximum range was required. They
argued that guns of a single calibre
would have similar characteristics
and could be salvo-fired by a single
director, giving corrections as
appropriate. Like most ideas, this
was not new. In particular, the
Italian, Cuniberti, had long pro-
pounded it and both Italian and
Japanese designs had hinted at it,
but it was its application by the
Americans with their South Carolinas that forced the British hand.

The latter had not been caught
napping for the Admiralty,
embodied in the person of the
dynamic 'Jackie' Fisher, had
already long since formed a com-
mittee to formulate proposals. In
1905 the resulting ship was laid
down. Her name was *Dreadnought*.

above
Typifying the armoured cruiser concept,
the U.S.S. *Brooklyn* of 1895 has her main
battery disposed in both centreline and
wing turrets and mixed secondary
armament in casemates. She served as
Schley's flagship at the defeat of a
Spanish Squadron off Santiago, Cuba in
1898.

below
The Japanese pre-Dreadnought
Shikishima was completed in a British
yard in 1899. Armed with four 12-inch
guns in turrets and fourteen 6-inch in
casements, she was to play an important
part in Togo's defeat of the Russians at
Tsushima in 1905.

Dreadnought and Beyond
the capital ship in the 20th century

Dreadnought was built in great secrecy in just one year and shipped the formidable armament of 10 12-inch guns in five twin turrets, three on the centreline and two sited in the waist. Her broadside was eight guns, but this was obtained more economically by the Americans, who superimposed twin turrets forward and aft, losing out only in the dubious benefits of chase fire. *Dreadnought*'s director control was sited atop a large tripod, inconveniently close · to the forward funnel. Her speed of 21 knots was achieved by the 23,000 shp developed by the first major steam turbine installation. These power units occupied far less space than the 16,500 shp triple-expansion engines in the contemporary 18-knot Lord Nelsons.

Her lack of secondary armament proved a drawback but, whatever *Dreadnought*'s faults, she marked a watershed in design that made all other battleships appear over-complex and leaden-footed. With the Russian fleet depleted, France more interested in smaller classes, and the growing power of Japan and the U.S. conveniently distant, Germany was the clear threat. A rumoured all-big-gun 'S' class never materialised and a baker's dozen of battleships built in the previous 5 years were quite outdated. Every capital ship was now, simply, Dreadnought or pre-Dreadnought.

The British, of course, also had a replacement problem and put nine more in the water in the next 4 years. All had 10 12-inch guns and the main improvement was in the general provision of secondary

FRANK WOOD

above

Dreadnought of 1906 was not perfect but opened a new, and final, phase in the story of the battleship. Her construction was typical of the British Admiralty's traditional response to a foreign stimulus.

opposite, top

Considering their status as obsolete pre-Dreadnoughts, the Canopus class battleships had an eventful war. *Canopus*, shown here, barely – and fortunately – missed Coronel but 'opened the bowling' at the Falklands. Here sisters *Goliath* and *Ocean* were both sunk at the Dardanelles.

opposite, lower

Among the finest battleships ever built were *Bismarck* and her sister *Tirpitz* In spite of their proven combat excellence, however, they belonged to a German fleet geared to commerce destruction.

armament and the adoption of partial superimposition in the *Neptune* in 1909. By contrast, the American Carolinas took 3 years to build and did not have turbines. The German Westfalens, too, still had reciprocating machinery and 12 11-inch guns in twin mountings. They had limited bunker space, giving a small radius of action, which convinced the British that they were intended for a war close to home. A 'two-keels-for-one' policy was pursued and a headlong race developed.

As effective gun range increased, the tendency was to incorporate more horizontal protection as a safeguard against plunging fire. In addition, *Neptune* was the first to have an upper deck strengthened against aerial attack.

The Americans put steam turbines into the North Dakotas and Utahs, and the Wyomings of 1910 increased the main battery to 12

12-inch guns. The Germans, not to be out-done, discarded their favourite 11-inch weapons for 12's in the Helgolands. They were all immediately eclipsed by the British Orions of 1912, which introduced the 13.5-inch gun and were partially oil-fired. The 13.5-inch gun was not so much 'one-upmanship' as a measure to give the projectile a lower muzzle velocity and extra weight to improve ballistics and impact effect.

As already noted, the French were uncharacteristically slow to join the all-big-gun club and the 1907 Dantons, with their mixed armament of only four 12-inch and 12 9.4's, were essentially pre-Dreadnought. The Jean Barts of 1910, however, adopted turbine propulsion and 12 12-inch guns, followed by the three Normandies with 10 13.4's to rival the Orions.

The Italians, always capable of interesting design, introduced the

71

triple turret, putting four into the
odd-looking *Dante Alighieri* of
1909. Her smallish displacement of
20,000 tons made superimposition
impossible and reduced the effectiveness of this battery. This was
partially rectified in the following
Giulio Cesares by superfiring
triples with twins.

The space-saving triple turret
was received enthusiastically and
featured on the Austro-Hungarian
Viribus Unitis class, the Russian
Marats and the later Impera-
tritsa Marias. The Americans
adopted the 14-inch gun in the

27,400-ton New Yorks together
with a temporary reversion to
reciprocating machinery. Their layout established a pattern followed
by succeeding classes, and armour
followed the all-or-nothing principle, concentrated on the protection of the vitals.

Japan was like France in being
slow to build. The two 22,000-ton
Kawachi's laid down in 1909 had
12 12-inch guns but badly arranged
in non-superimposed twin mountings. By 1913, however, the two
Yamashiros jumped to 31,000 tons
with four triple 14-inch turrets.

The Germans retained their 12-
inch gun for the Kaisers and
Königs, which were commissioned
1912–15, though rumour in British
circles credited them during construction with 14-inch weapons.
Had their protection been
improved they would indeed have
been formidable but they caused
the Royal Navy to jump from 13.5-
inch guns to 15-inch.

For comparison, a German 12-
inch projectile weighed about 900
lb against the 1,400 lb of a British
13.5. The new 15-inch averaged
over 1,900 lb and the Germans were

totally outclassed, particularly as Vickers developed one of their most excellent guns to complement the projectile, ranging out to better than 35,000 yards. The carriers of these weapons were the five Queen Elizabeths, without doubt the finest battleships of the era. They carried eight 15-inch guns on a full load displacement of around 33,000 tons and could make 24 knots on 75,000 shp. They were the first battleships to be fired exclusively by oil which, besides its convenience, greatly diminished the smoke nuisance. They were followed by the similarly armed but slightly smaller quintet of Revenges. These sacrificed some speed for better protection and had anti-torpedo bulges. Having fewer boilers (18 against 24) their uptakes were trunked into a single funnel of impressive proportions.

Although the British had overestimated the speed of German gun development the smoke that they had scented did indeed presage a fire, for the Germans were jumping from 12-inch guns, not to 14, but to 15-inch at a stroke. These were

top
Although the appearance of the *Suffren* of 1899 was less extreme than some French designs, her armament of four 12-inch and ten 6.5-inch guns was obsolete after 1906. She was active at the Dardanelles as Guépratte's flagship.

above
The German König-class battleship *Grosser Kurfürst*, completed in 1914. Note the volume of smoke produced by the coal-burner, uncluttered layout, casemated secondary armament and air-recognition symbol on 'B' turret.

installed in the two Badens, which did not enter service until 1916. Remarkably similar to the 'QEs' they carried an almost identical armament on a shorter, but beamier, hull. Their protection was no better than their British equivalents but they were far more thoroughly sub-divided.

Lacking modern combat experience the Royal Navy went into the First World War largely believing that it would be the same as 100 years earlier – the reduction of the enemy's power by the slow strangulation of blockade, keeping the main Battle Fleet ready for a sort of Armageddon when 'they' dared to come out, when overwhelming might would decide the day.

Two events rapidly shattered these rather cosy assumptions. Three armoured cruisers were sunk together by one German submarine and the new battleship *Audacious* was lost after striking only one mine. These two comparatively cheap weapons – the submarine and the mine – challenged unseen the might of the big gun and rendered the old methods of close investment of the enemy impossible.

For Jellicoe's Grand Fleet battleships, the war was hardly action packed. The bases of the German High Seas Fleet under Scheer were only 10 hours steaming distance from the English east coast. The Germans, inferior in numbers, adopted a 'fleet-in-being' approach, and posed a continuous threat that kept the Royal Navy permanently waiting, and unable to ignore it. The British unsuccessfully adopted aggressive patrolling to entice the enemy out but spent most of their time exercising to achieve a high pitch of efficiency. Their margin of superiority over their enemy, however, was not sufficient for them to take chances.

Scheer, on the other hand, used tactics such as the bombardment of English coastal towns to bring out elements of the Grand Fleet to where they could be ambushed by submarines or superior surface forces. But Jellicoe was guided by too good an intelligence system to be caught in this manner and something akin to a stalemate developed.

Somewhat paradoxically, it was the older British pre-Dreadnoughts that saw the early action. At the commencement of the ill-fated cam-

above
The battle fleet gathering on the eve of the Coronation Review of George V in 1911 was one remoulded around a powerful nucleus of dreadnought battleships and cruisers.

opposite, top
A German Kaiser-class battleship fires a 12-inch broadside during the First World War. The five 24,000-tonners of this group had a layout modelled upon that of the British Neptunes. Note the casemated 5.9-inch secondary armament.

opposite, lower
H.M.S. *Iron Duke* in 1917. Her class was derived from the similar KGV's and formed the basis of the design of the successful Queen Elizabeths. Note the armament of ten 13.5-inch guns in five twin turrets and the aircraft on 'B' turret.

paign to take Constantinople, 16 old French and British battleships were given the job of forcing the Dardanelles in the teeth of gunfire from the forts and Mahan's dictum that ships are no match for prepared coastal defences. They achieved a surprising measure of success with little loss from Turkish gunfire but, upon withdrawing temporarily, no less than three British ships became victims of a line of only 20 mines. The fleet withdrew to support the army from the open sea but lost another three battleships, one to a destroyer's torpedoes and two to those of a submarine. The mine and torpedo had again beaten the gun and the fleet retired to safer waters and the campaign atrophied.

It is to be regretted that this large pool of old battleships was not used more imaginatively. Taking the view that they were expendable anyway, how much more effective would one have been at, say, the blocking of Zeebrugge. Thick armour and great close-range fire power, a light ship with minimum bunkers and stores, and the result should have been unquestionable.

The 'First Division', having watched everybody else in action

for too long, eventually had its chance at Jutland in May 1916. Losses in British capital ships were confined to battlecruisers and only one German pre-Dreadnought was sunk, by a destroyer's torpedo in a close-range mêlée.

In spite of the disappointing outcome of the action, some lessons emerged. The fast, heavy-gunned battleships of the Queen Elizabeth

class proved their value by moving in to the relief of the hard-pressed battlecruisers, which the rather fool-hardy Beatty had committed too heavily. They took and dispensed tremendous punishment but their design was sound and they survived. The full range of their 15-inch guns could not be exploited because of poor visibility, but their hitting power and accuracy,

above
The powerful fleet of the Kaiser was reinforced on its southern flank by that of the Austro-Hungarian Empire. This not-inconsiderable force is seen here, led in 1912 by its new flagship *Viribus Unitis*, the first of four dreadnoughts which introduced superimposed triple turrets.

left, centre
The heavy menace of a battle squadron is well captured in this impression of British dreadnoughts in 1914.

left, lower
Although the Army was landed largely in the traditional way using ship's boats, the Gallipoli operation saw also the introduction of specialised craft for amphibious landings.

opposite, top
The French battleship *Suffren* wearing the flag of Admiral Guépratte, senior officer of the French squadron at the Dardanelles in 1915.

together with their flat trajectory, established them as the best major-calibre guns yet produced.

In spite of legend, German armour at Jutland was pierced far more frequently than British, but the former's sub-division and better attention to detail gave them superior 'survivability', improved further by the tendency for British shells to break up on contact. The Grand Fleet's continual exercising paid off in generally better gunnery, but, again, this could not be exploited in the low visibility, where the Germans' superior ranging techniques usually put their salvoes on the target far more quickly.

A contributory factor to the lack of result in the battle was the poor British signalling, an all-too-common failing. Jellicoe, often with only the haziest notion of the situation, played safe and, when given the chance, manoeuvred like the master that he was. Possibly his greatest error was the battle-turn-away on being threatened by a German destroyer torpedo attack; Dewey's earlier advice, 'Damn the

torpedoes', should have been taken in pressing home a fading advantage. Jellicoe, a cautious man, was only too aware of the consequences of defeat and, for all his qualities, was no Nelson. The acceptance of higher losses at Jutland, as well as at the forcing of the Dardanelles, could well have produced results of incalculable worth.

The Grand Fleet was not to get another chance and, although in even more overwhelming strength after reinforcement by an American squadron late in 1917, was unable to exert its will directly. The High Seas Fleet attempted one more major sortie and then lapsed into a torpor of inaction which destroyed it from within as its morale slowly crumbled. Its end – revolution, internment and scuttling at Scapa – was ignoble and undeserved, but it had been destroyed by slow pressure even as the French of over a century before. It proved that a 'fleet-in-being' approach to war could never achieve a victory; at best, it could only stave off a defeat.

The Americans' war-time pro-gramme wisely concentrated on

more urgently needed classes than battleships. Although the two Pennsylvanias were completed during the war, the five Californias and Idahos arrived too late to see action. Construction in them was simplified by a standardisation of armament to 12 14-inch guns in triple turrets and an 'all-or-nothing' system of protection. Their turbo-electric machinery was interesting, with steam turbines driving generators which powered motors geared to the shafts. It was complex but needed no gearbox, and conferred great flexibility of control.

After the Armistice, Britain found herself in naval competition with her late Allies. Precipitated by America and Japan eyeing each other over the vast wastes of the Pacific, the new race gathered a frightening momentum. The U.S. Navy adopted the 16-inch gun and embarked on a programme of 10 battleships and six battlecruisers in answer to the Japanese plan to build a class of 45,000-tonners with eight 18-inch guns. Britain, faced with the prospect of losing her naval supremacy, was forced to

reply with planned 48,500-ton ships with nine 18-inch guns, an exceedingly large jump from the recently completed Revenges.

The impossible economics of these grandiose plans forced the rivals to the conference table, resulting in agreement and the Washington Treaty of 1922. Amongst other clauses, this limited individual battleships to 16-inch guns on a tonnage not exceeding 35,000. These parameters were arrived at primarily to allow the U.S. Navy to complete its new Marylands. The Japanese retained their Nagatos but the larger Kagas passed, with all the rest of the plans, into oblivion.

Another agreement was on strict ratios of tonnages between signatories. As a result Britain sent no less than 22 post-Dreadnoughts to the breakers, compared with four ships of the American navy.

As is the way of things, Britain, having sent so many fine ships to premature ends, was allowed to build two more. These were the Nelsons which re-introduced the 16-inch gun in new triple turrets. Their 'bob-tailed' appearance is often wrongly ascribed to a lopping under the terms of the Treaty. In practice, it was just a device to give the maximum of protection over the smallest area. Further weight was saved on machinery by the adoption of super-heated steam propulsion.

The major navies took advantage of the breathing-space afforded by the Treaty to modernise thoroughly many existing battleships. The British QE's were given the first of several facelifts and the Americans and Japanese were also busy, but none compared with the Italian Cavours, which were not only re-armed but also lengthened and re-engined, emerging as virtually new ships.

As the nations got over their post-war problems, more money was available and old rivalries re-emerged. Germany, allowed to build within limits, followed the interesting Deutschlands with the two Scharnhorsts which, although rather lightly armed with 11-inch guns, were excellent fast battleships whose steam turbines were complemented by cruising diesels to improve their range for commerce raiding. France, inevitably, was stung to retaliate and produced her pair of Strasbourgs. These followed the Nelson design to the extent that all eight 13-inch guns were concentrated into two quadruple turrets, making a central armoured citadel possible, which enclosed all vitals in the smallest weight of thick armour.

This caused a Mediterranean unbalance which encouraged the Italians to lay down the two large Littorio's (later followed by a third). Never ones for adhering too strictly to treaty limitations, the Italians packed nine 15-inch guns

H.M.S. "HOOD" V "BISMARCK"
24.5.1941

above
The greatest weakness of the battle cruiser *Hood* was in her horizontal protection. It proved fatal in her long-range duel with the *Bismarck*, whose plunging 15-inch shells penetrated all too easily.

opposite, top
Strasbourg and her sister *Dunkerque* were a pair of fast French battleships which incorporated the same central citadel protection as the British Nelsons. Their eight 13-inch guns were mounted forward in two quadruple turrets.

opposite, lower
The American battleship *Washington* was one of the first pair designed subsequent to the abandonment of the Washington Treaty. They introduced a standardised main armament of nine 16-inch guns.

right
H.M.S. *Nelson*, seen from her sister *Rodney*. The odd 'all-forward' layout was dictated largely by the desire to incorporate the thickest armour over the smallest area. Their design owed much to the '1921 battle cruisers' which were never built, but they suffered from a low speed.

into elegant hulls of over 41,000 tons. The arms spiral continued with the French reply of four Richelieus, though only two were actually completed and were extensions of the Strasbourg design, but with eight 15-inch guns.

Meanwhile the Japanese and Americans were involved in a race of their own. Where the Italians and Germans at least paid lip-service to limitations, the Japanese ignored them totally. The American policy was never to build warships that could not pass throught the Panama Canal. Taking the lock dimensions at their parameters, the Japanese calculated that 60,000 tons was the theoretical maximum size. With permitted armament of nine 16-inch guns,

this would leave margins for a speed of about 23 knots. With none of the restrictions that affected the Americans, the three Japanese Yamatos were to be of 70,000 tons and reach 28 knots, and would have the incredible number of nine 18-inch guns, each throwing a 3,200 lb projectile (compared with the 2,250 lb missile of a 16-inch). The comparatively short and beamy hull enabled armour up to 22 inches in thickness to be used.

America, now convinced of Japanese perfidy, laid down six Washingtons and South Dakotas in 1937–39. These 16-inch-gun ships re-introduced the steam turbine and were followed by the New Jerseys of 1941. No longer treaty-bound, these displaced

45,000 tons to give the necessary length for the incorporation of machinery to develop power for an unprecedented 35 knots.

The Germans and British were, predictably, again in competition, with the former in the opening stages of their 'Plan Z', masterminded by Admiral Raeder, which was to provide a powerful and balanced fleet capable of challenging the Royal Navy by 1944. The two Bismarcks of 1936 reintroduced the 15-inch gun and were large at nearly 53,000 tons full load, but were only to be an intermediate stage before the coming of the 64,000-ton Friedrich der Grosse class. These would have been propelled by multi-unit diesel installations but they were overtaken by events and never completed.

Britain still doggedly adhered to the agreed limitations, to which she built the five King George V class. They adopted the 14-inch gun for a better balanced armament, but the planned 12 guns had to be reduced to 10 to enable armour on a proper scale to be provided. Two quadruple turrets were shipped – new to the R.N. – the forward one superfired by a twin. The class was not completed until after the outbreak of war but this was because Britain had, like Japan, correctly assessed the likely importance of air power at sea and had put much effort into aircraft carrier construction.

With the Lions which followed, limitations were finally abandoned. Had these ships been completed, they would have looked like triple-turreted KG Vs. One of the reasons for their demise was the lack of 16-inch guns and an interesting one-off was the lone *Vanguard*, designed rapidly to make use of available 15-inch turrets of First World War vintage and taken out of *Glorious* and *Courageous* on their conversions to carriers.

Battleships played a smaller part in the Second World War than in the First. Far fewer in numbers, they often formed the nucleus of a balanced carrier group. This practice was established successfully by the British Force H in the Mediterranean in 1940, but brought to perfection by the Japanese and Americans in the Pacific later.

The early loss of the *Royal Oak* whilst at anchor was a sharp reminder of the vulnerability of battleships to submarine attack. The rest of the class spent the war largely on convoy protection; they saw comparatively little action as a result, but their presence saved many a convoy from attack by surface raiders. It should be remembered that the Germans, like all of Britain's enemies in history, appreciated the vulnerability of her commerce and geared their efforts toward its destruction.

Warspite was used boldly at Second Narvik in 1940 in support of light forces, far inside enemy waters, echoing the spirit of Beatty at Heligoland Bight. It was the

beginning of a busy war for the modernised QE's. Used skilfully in company with aircraft carriers, they established a complete ascendency over the Italian fleet. Matapan in 1941 showed a new appetite for night-fighting, so sadly lacking at Jutland.

The action followed the delaying of the Italian fleet by a carrier strike and the German *Bismarck* was similarly brought to book. Her sinking also involved the use of destroyers in classic torpedo attacks, which, though carried out at night were largely unsuccessful, due partly to the use by the Germans of radar-laid guns. This new aid had also enabled British cruisers to dog *Bismarck*'s every move. Fought to a standstill by 14 and 16-inch gunfire, she proved extraordinarily difficult to sink, due mainly to the short ranges giving the British projectiles a flat trajectory, so that they had to pierce the thick vertical armour.

Those who had prophesied the battleship's helplessness in the face of air attack seemed to be wrong for a while. *Barham* was lost to a determined submarine attack in November 1941; *Queen Elizabeth* and *Valiant* were then put out of the war for a considerable time by explosions caused by Italian frogmen, an unforeseen method of attack used to great effect by the individualistic Italian Navy.

Only a few days before, however, Japan had entered the war, and suddenly the 'air-school' was vindicated at Pearl Harbor. As at

Taranto, the battleships at Pearl Harbor were caught at their moorings, but it is a measure of the extent to which the type had already declined that the Americans considered themselves fortunate to have lost them rather than their carriers, which were at sea. This overwhelming attack had been mounted by a carrier group, and the carrier became the new queen of the seas with a striking power which left the battleship out-classed and soon relegated to a consort role. This lesson was again soon brutally underlined by the sinking of the *Repulse* and *Prince of Wales* under saturation air attack.

The 'conventional' sinking of the *Scharnhorst* and *Kirishima* did little to change the new role of the battleship and the Pacific War developed into a series of fluid actions between opposing carrier groups. The accompanying battleships were there to meet attack by enemy equivalents but were primarily to lend massive A/A support from the myriad short-range automatic weapons they now carried. Main calibre bombardments became increasingly directed at shore targets.

The American assault against Leyte at the end of 1944 provoked the last great actions with the remaining Japanese fleet. The *Yamato*'s great sister, *Musashi*, was sunk by aerial attack but, fittingly two more were sunk by night gunnery alone. The final radar-laid salvo from the *Mississippi* into the stricken *Yamashiro* was the last act of battleship against battleship.

Faded stars with no more major roles to play, allied battleships found themselves used primarily as gun support for amphibious landings. Many had paid off by the close of the war to release their trained crews for more vital craft. Most were soon scrapped. Employment was found for some in the Korean War but not against their own kind. The end of the long time of British 'battlers' came with the scrapping of *Vanguard* in 1960. The Americans hung on to their four Iowas, of which the *New Jersey* took part in her third war, this time in Vietnam.

A reprieve was possible through experiments in firing fin-stabilised, non-rotating, rocket-assisted projectiles from large smooth-bore guns but these proved to lack the accuracy of a guided missile, which enabled the same fire power (albeit with less flexibility) to be packed into a far smaller hull. It was the end for the battleship; the submarine had proved her vulnerable and aircraft had finally dethroned her.

The air threat in the Second World War resulted in major units becoming festooned with a multitude of 40 and 20mm automatic guns. Here, a quadruple 40mm mounting has been added above the open 5-inch weapons of the U.S.S. *Arkansas*.

The Battle Cruiser
an idea looking for a role

Only a year after *Dreadnought* went down the ways, she was followed by H.M.S. *Invincible*. As the first Battle Cruiser she was, in many ways, more revolutionary than her predecessor. The concept was simply to put the armament of a battleship in a lighter hull, relying on speed for protection. Battle cruisers were designed to act as a fast wing to the main fleet – a sort of seaborne cavalry – and, more specifically, to eclipse the armoured cruiser. As the latter were in the same size bracket as the battleship, so was the 'Dreadnought-cruiser' akin to her namesake. The required extra four knots was achieved only at the expense of some 75 per cent increase in power, a longer hull, one turret less and greatly reduced protection. In the latter, they had been foreshadowed by several classes, notably the Italian Lepantos of 1883, and the more recent Japanese Tsukuba and Italian Regina Elena classes.

As if unconvinced of the battle cruisers' value, the major navies did not immediately react, except that is, the Germans, who were badly misled and laid down *Blücher* before *Invincible*, was launched. She was really no more than a fast, oversized armoured cruiser, with only 8.2-inch guns. Rapidly realising their error, they laid down the *Von der Tann* in 1907. Longer and beamier than the British ships, she achieved 28 knots on trials and, by limiting the armament to only eight 11-inch guns, she could afford a greater degree of protection and subdivision. Where the British made scarcely any improvements in producing the Indefatigables, the German Moltkes had an extra

superimposed turret aft and were obviously of so much better a design that the British were stung to reply with the Lions. About 110 feet longer and of almost twice the power, they could easily maintain 28 knots and shipped 13.5-inch guns. They were followed by the lone, magnificent, *Tiger*, in which power was further increased by 50 per cent to 108,000 shp; she was a first cousin to the Japanese *Kongo*, built in Britain.

Faced with this competition the Germans increased calibre to 12-inch and size to around 28,000 tons in the Derfflingers. Their more modest speed and armament again permitted better protection.

The First World War began well for the battle cruiser as a result of the Heligoland Bight affair, where British light forces, sweeping the

Beatty's flagship *Lion* at the Dogger Bank action. In spite of the greater part of the German force being allowed to escape, the image of the battle cruiser remained untarnished until Jutland.

area to establish an early initiative, were rudely set upon by superior enemy forces and, in a series of actions in poor visibility, were hard pressed. Then Beatty's battle cruisers, acting as distant heavy cover, dashed into these highly dangerous waters and turned the tables decisively.

Three months later, after the defeat of Cradock's scratch squadron by von Spee's armoured cruisers at Coronel, *Inflexible* and *Invincible* were detached from the Grand Fleet to intercept the Ger-

man force which, having escaped the fall of Tsingtau, was making its way home. They were duly apprehended at the Falklands. In perfect weather, the speed and superior gun calibre of the British enabled them to dictate the action. Both of the enemy armoured cruisers were despatched by deliberate fire from long range. The ammunition expenditure was high but the tactics were correct. Defeat had been avenged and the new legend was born. So great were the hopes pinned upon the type that the next two, the Renowns, were rushed into production, introducing the 15-inch gun.

The still unblooded German battle cruisers then commenced a series of tip-and-run raids, bombarding English east-coast towns to entice Royal Naval forces out to where they could be ambushed by superior strength. With their speed coupled with a head start, they were as unlikely to be intercepted as were the French back in the Napoleonic Wars and before, but in January 1915 on the Dogger Bank, they were caught out by Beatty. A long stern chase developed with the superior speed and calibre of the British ships slowly telling. The German tailender was the hybrid *Blücher*, which was severely mauled without being able to reply. The force would, undoubtedly, have suffered further loss if Beatty's *Lion* had not been damaged. In falling out of line, she signalled to the effect that the action should be pressed home, but it was misread and only the *Blücher* was despatched. This led to consider-

able public criticism at the time.

In the course of the action a 13.5-inch shell from *Lion* pierced the barbette armour of *Seydlitz*. The range was 17,500 yards and the projectile struck at a very steep angle, exploding in the handling space of the after turret. Ready-to-use charges ignited, the flash spreading the fire to the neighbouring turret. Only prompt flooding of the magazines saved the ship, and as a result improved isolation of charges was introduced to all German capital ships, a move that was to stand them in good stead.

At Jutland, in May 1916, both sides used their battle cruiser squadrons as a fast wing of the fleet and they were engaged in fierce action with each other to prevent fleet deployment being observed. The British advantage of six to five was squandered by faulty signalling, which lead to one German ship being left unmarked. The heavier British guns were used at shortish ranges but Hipper's ships had the best of it. Beatty was extricated by the new Queen Elizabeths, which had the speed to engage. *Lion* had already been hard hit and suffered a flash explosion, which she survived by magazine flooding. *Queen Mary* was then hit and disintegrated, apparently from a similar cause. Two more British battle cruisers were to be sunk in similar circumstances that day but only one German, the latter's turret armour being pierced on about 10 occasions.

The fleet's triple loss can be ascribed to design defects, faulty

below
The aftermath of Jutland. *Seydlitz* demonstrates the ability of the German battle cruiser to absorb heavy action damage and survive.

signalling which left unmarked opponents to shoot undisturbed, and operating too close to the main battle line. Hipper's success was due to excellent range-finding techniques putting their salvoes rapidly on to their targets and to the ability of his ships to absorb punishment.

The two Renowns, then completing, had extra armour worked in above their magazines in an apparently faulty assessment of the Jutland losses. The 15-inch gun was also mounted in the 'tin-clads' *Glorious* and *Courageous*. These were 22,700-ton, 33-knot vessels of very shallow draught, designed for Fisher's proposed naval operations in the Baltic. The third of the class, *Furious*, was slightly enlarged and designed to mount a couple of 18-inch weapons in single turrets. The rate of fire of these monster guns was so low that it is difficult to envisage the ship in any sort of fight. They hardly saw action in their original form and were known to the fleet as the Spurious, Curious and Outrageous, names that describe them adequately.

All this work with heavy guns inspired the Germans to embark on three 15-inch gunned 34,000-tonners. Britain was by now building four Hoods, but the German building effort was not up to the extra demand and their ships were cancelled soon after commencement. Similarly, three of the British vessels were abandoned, only the *Hood* being completed in 1920, as her construction was well advanced. This extraordinarily handsome ship took into account lessons learned at Jutland, her protection being on a par with the QE's. The 144,000 shp required for her 32 knots, resulted in a very long 42,000-ton hull, but a mistake was to spread the armour too far, instead of using it on the 'all-or-nothing' principle. Much later this was to prove fatal. She incorporated small tube boilers and used superheated steam to keep down the machinery weight.

After the scuttling of the High Seas Fleet at Scapa, the British battle cruisers were alone in the world with the exception of the Japanese *Kongo*. The Americans were constructing the Lexingtons and announced that these would be followed by six Constellations of 43,000 tons, armed with 16-inch guns. The rather similar Japanese Akagi class were to be followed by a class of 45,000-tonners mounting eight 18-inch weapons! The British responded to the challenge with plans for the quartette of '1921 battle cruisers', mounting nine 16-inch guns on a 48,000-ton displacement. Three triple turrets, close-spaced, would have enabled excellent protection to be incorporated.

These plans, like others, were cancelled after the Washington Treaty, but they greatly influenced the design of the Nelson-class battleships. One clause of the Treaty stated that an agreed percentage of capital ship tonnage be scrapped or converted. The latter alternative was taken by the British, Americans and Japanese in converting battle cruisers to prototype fast carriers.

The type had already been largely superseded by the fast battleship, though of them the French Strasbourgs of 1932 and the German Scharnhorsts of 1934 came close to the ideal.

By the Second World War, the battle cruiser had out-lived her original roles and entered a conflict that was out of her class. In May 1941, the *Hood* was successfully vectored on to her quarry through a classic 'track-and-report' cruiser operation. But she faced no armoured cruiser; the formidable *Bismarck* destroyed her with magnificent gunnery at long range, the plunging 15-inch projectiles easily piercing the *Hood's* limited horizontal protection. She was accompanied by the brand new *Prince of Wales* battleship, and her last signal as senior ship was 'Conform to my movements'. The correct tactics would have been to

separate and split the enemy's fire as was done by Harwood at the River Plate. This last gasp of the 'Line of Battle' philosophy had proved as disastrous as ever.

When it might finally have been thought that the battle cruiser was spent, the Americans produced a trio of Alaskas, very much like 12-inch-gunned Scharnhorsts. The pair completed were never used as planned and, with their demolition, the type died.

top
Built to counter a faulty appreciation of Britain's first battle cruiser, the German *Blücher* was armed with an 8.2-inch main battery. She was totally outgunned and sunk at the Dogger Bank in 1915.

above
One of the final trio of German battle cruisers, armed with 12-inch guns, *Derfflinger* suffered an unworthy end at Scapa in 1919.

Naval Aviation
the giants displaced

The sea battle, like its counterpart on land, was often won – or avoided – by a commander with better Intelligence than his enemy. Not even the keenest eye could penetrate beyond the horizon and, in the pre-radio days, the 'eyes' of the fleet were first of all fast sailing frigates then, later, the cruiser squadrons. An obvious way of improving observation was to have an eye in the sky. Although, by the turn of the century, heavier-than-air machines were staggering into the clouds, they were of negligible use and the most reliable means of obtaining lift for anything was to tow a kite behind a fast ship steaming into the wind. Early experiments with kites started in the Royal Navy in 1903, but it was 1908 before brave men went aloft in them. This lack of urgency was probably due to the radio-fitted airship looking a better proposition. A dirigible was bought in 1909 by the Navy for experiments, but it crashed on trials and the idea was abandoned in favour of small, towed observation balloons.

Meanwhile the American, French and Russian navies were exploring the greater potential of the now more reliable powered aircraft. The U.S. Navy took first honours when Eugene Ely flew in a Curtiss biplane from a temporary platform on the bows of the anchored cruiser *Birmingham*. On this occasion he had to land ashore but, shortly afterwards, landed on the after end of the *Pennsylvania*. His aircraft speed was arrested by sandbag-weighted lines across the deck, but the great significance of Ely's feat was largely ignored as

The American carrier *Hornet* launches B-52's in Doolittle's famous Tokyo raid of April 1942. The raid accomplished small material damage but served early notice to the Japanese that, like Pearl Harbor few places were secure against seaborne airpower.

the navy began exploring the use of seaplanes.

The Germans were more interested in supporting their fleet with their large, rigid Zeppelins and left the British to continue the American's practical approach with wheeled aircraft. In 1912 flights were made from platforms on the battleships *Africa* and *Hibernia* and were sufficiently encouraging to lead to a more permanent platform on the forward end of the cruiser *Hermes*. However, the problem was the recovery of land aircraft after such flights and interest shifted to seaplanes, which could drop bombs and torpedoes as well as observe for the fleet. *Hermes* was an early war casualty and was succeeded by the ex-Cunard liner *Campania*, which put seaplanes into the air from rail-guided trolleys on a forward flight-deck, which was served

by an elevator. They were expected to land back on the sea and be recovered by crane. She could have made history with their use at Jutland, but failed to sail on time because of yet another misunderstanding in signals. It was left to the little converted cross-Channel packet, *Engadine*, to fly-off the first aircraft at a naval action.

In 1915 the Americans had another 'first' by putting an aircraft up from a catapult on the *North Carolina*. The superfluous 18-inch-gunned *Furious* was com-

opposite, top
Before the arrestor hook. Fine judgement on the part of both pilot and deck party were necessary for the safe landing of this Sopwith Pup aboard H.M.S. *Furious.*

opposite, lower
H.M.S. *Empress* was one of a group of cross-channel packets converted to seaplane carriers. Her near-sister, *Engadine*, was the first to operate aircraft at a naval action.

below
The carrying of scout planes by major fleet units was discontinued eventually, largely because of the great fire hazard that they posed. A Kingfisher float plane is seen on its catapult in this 1944 view of the American battleship *Arkansas.*

pleted with a *Campania*-style flying-off deck forward. Later the after turret was removed to make way for a complementary flying-on deck. The superstructure, still complete, caused severe problems with turbulence and the obvious answer was to substitute a straight-through flight deck. An incomplete liner hull was topped-off thus, completing as H.M.S. *Argus*, whose name suggests an observation, rather than an attack role. She had no superstructure, and uptakes exhausted over the side; she was the world's first true aircraft carrier. She commissioned in 1918 and was followed after 2 years by *Eagle*, built on a battleship hull and featuring an island superstructure and arrestor wires. The principle was established and *Hermes II* was completed in 1923 as the first carrier built as such from the keel up. It remained only for *Furious* finally to get the 'full treatment' and Britain had a quartette which put her ahead of the world in naval aviation.

The Japanese, too, took the carrier seriously and completed the *Hosho* soon after the *Hermes* entered service. Her small superstructure was soon removed, setting the fashion for many later Japanese carriers. The U.S. Navy at this time had only the *Langley*, a converted collier.

The Washington Treaty gave a fillip to carrier development by allowing the conversion of capital ships, which otherwise would have had to be broken up. Britain, Japan and the United States each converted a brace of battle cruisers successfully, but the French rebuilt the battleship *Béarn,* which proved too slow. The powerful machinery of the others conferred high speeds. The British *Glorious* and *Furious* could make 30 knots but were dwarfed by the two American *Lexingtons*, which were each dominated by enormous stacks, the casings of which encompassed the five uptakes of the original design.

The Japanese embarked upon the conversion of the *Akagi* and *Amagi* but, after the latter was heavily damaged on the slip by an earthquake, the battleship *Kaga* was substituted. All became well known and provided the basis of experience for the new generation of construction in the 1930s.

The Americans and Japanese, still deeply suspicious of each other, built quickly to the permitted limits. The early *Ranger* proved too small and was followed by the *Enterprise* and *Yorktown*, whose

vast capacity for aircraft has since been a feature of U.S. carriers. They were 34-knot ships and of only some 20,000 tons, but stowed about 80 aircraft as against the 60 of the similar-sized *Hiryu* and *Soryu*, which had followed the little *Ryujo*. The Hiryus were completed in 1937, just before the British *Ark Royal*. The famous 'Ark' was strongly built, with the hangar walls continuing the main hull structure up to the flight deck. Interestingly, the Americans had used this form of construction in the Lexingtons but reverted to the system of adding hangar and flight-deck to a self-contained hull. The Japanese, too, used this method but the British retained the integral construction. It reduced their aircraft capacity a little but permitted an armoured flight-deck and hangar walls to be incorporated.

With the abandonment of the Washington Treaty limitations, the British built the four Illustrious class. Having only one hangar against the *Ark*'s two, they had a smaller capacity and lower silhouette. The following pair of Implacables reversed this.

In 1937, Japan laid down the splendid pair of Shokakus and then, somewhat tardily, the expanding Reichsmarine started on the two 23,000-ton Graf Zeppelins. Having different requirements, the Germans produced a design aimed at commerce raiding which was really a large cruiser with facilities for operating some 40 aircraft. The powerful armament of 16 5.9-inch and 12 4.1-inch guns contrasted with the 16 4.7-inch of British

practice. Neither was completed, due to inter-service rivalries rather than any technological failings. No satisfactory arrestor system was ever developed and no specialist naval aircraft. The planned complement of Ju 87D Stuka dive bombers and Bf 109G fighters would have found the going rough in competition with foreign front-line carriers.

Another land power, France, failed to comprehend the importance of the carrier. The *Joffre*, as successor to the unsatisfactory *Béarn*, was laid down too late and was broken up on the stocks after the fall of France in 1940.

The last major naval power in the rival camps was Italy. She assumed that she had no need of seaborne aviation as the whole of her major sphere of interest, the

Mediterranean, could be covered by land-based aircraft. After the coming of war, however, the British fleet carriers caused such mayhem that an urgent programme was begun to convert a fast liner hull into the 27,000-ton carrier *Aquila*, planned to carry 50 aircraft. Repeatedly damaged, she was never completed.

In the rapid build-up to war the Japanese, by conversions, managed to complete four carriers to one from America. The latter awoke to their position and, typically, put in hand the 25-strong Essex class. They featured the 'hangar-on-top' and their 100-aircraft capacity needed deck-edge elevators. These did not impinge on hangar space but, being more liable to damage and weakening the hull shell, they were never favoured by the British.

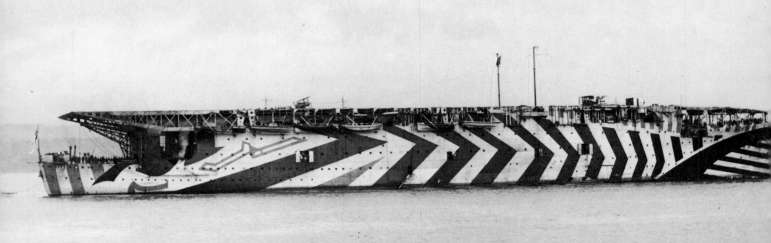

To the end of 1941, the sea war was a European affair and the Royal Navy used its carriers imaginatively, if not always successfully, against enemy fleets that had none. Anti-submarine operations were quickly instituted but, although the carrier eventually proved to be the answer, the units they operated were too large; the result was the sinking of *Courageous* and a near-miss on *Ark Royal*. They reverted to their proper role and, in quick succession, crippled the Italian fleet at Taranto and brought about the Battle of Matapan and the loss of *Bismarck* through airborne torpedo strikes. They also allowed the fleet to operate in areas previously dominated by hostile air power. This was not achieved without loss. *Glorious*, denuded of her aircraft, was sunk by surface attack off Norway; *Eagle* and *Ark Royal* were lost to submarines in the Mediterranean. *Illustrious* took a fearful beating from German dive-bombers off Malta. A more lightly-built carrier than the latter would have succumbed, but her thick flightdeck saved her and provided a lesson for all later designs.

opposite, top
The germ of the fast carrier group concept. *Ark Royal*, in company with *Renown* and *Southampton*, working out of Gibraltar in 1941.

opposite, lower
Dazzle-painted after the fashion much favoured during the First World War, the British aircraft carrier *Argus* was converted from the hull of an incomplete liner. Most early examples lacked an island superstructure, but only the Japanese persevered with the idea.

top
Destroyer *Legion* closes the sinking *Ark Royal* to take off survivors. Submarines accounted for the greatest number of British carrier losses in the Second World War.

right
The escort carrier was the key to victory in the Atlantic in the Second World War. This observer's-eye view of H.M.S. *Chaser* in 1942 shows the mercantile hull and distinctly limited facilities.

above
A Phantom is catapulted from H.M.S.
Ark Royal. The spiralling cost of
replacing strike carriers operating fixed
wing aircraft will probably result in their
extinction, in favour of smaller units
with helicopters and STOL aircraft.

left
The American carrier *Forrestal* was the
first to be constructed postwar and
incorporating improvements such as the
angled deck. As can be seen from the
photograph, this feature permits
simultaneous launch and recovery of
aircraft.

opposite
To strike first and to avoid being struck
is the aim of the carrier. Early
intelligence of an enemy's position is
therefore essential, and is supplied by
the long range radar of aircraft such as
the AEW Gannet, seen here.

The convoy war of 1941 was especially grim in mid-Atlantic, where existing air coverage could not reach. As a stop-gap answer, a captured German cargo liner was rebuilt by the British as the escort carrier *Audacity*. She had no hangar and carried only six aircraft, but in her short existence proved her value both in destroying enemy reconnaissance aircraft whose job it was to home submarines on to a convoy, and in keeping down submarines, frustrating their attack manoeuvres.

Realising the escort carrier's huge potential, the Americans' applied great resources to their series production. Early units were converted merchantmen but later ones were purpose-built, many serving under the White Ensign. A class of faster escort carriers was converted from cruiser hulls by the Americans for fleet use. Known variously as 'Woolworth' carriers or 'baby flat-tops', over 100 were completed and played a major part in the defeat of the U-boat.

Before the escort carriers entered service, the British used stopgaps such as the Merchant Aircraft Carriers, or MAC ships, merchantmen carrying a full cargo under their flightdecks, and Catapult Armed Merchantmen, or CAM ships. These were freighters with a catapult on their forecastle, from which a fighter aircraft was fired, usually a Hurricane. This dealt with an intruder and then 'ditched', the pilot being recovered from the sea.

In December 1941 a new type of war was ushered-in when 360 Japanese aircraft from six carriers suddenly hit Pearl Harbor in a pre-emptive strike inspired by Taranto. The American fleet was surprised and heavily mauled although its carriers were saved by being already at sea. The Japanese group then went on to ravage the ill-prepared British area of the Bay of Bengal. Amongst losses suffered was that of the veteran carrier *Hermes*.

The carrier group was ideally suited to a maritime war in the vast Pacific and the Japanese struck almost at will until the Americans rallied and surprised them at the Coral Sea. Each side lost a carrier

but the Japanese also lost many experienced aircrew and did not achieve their objective.

Midway was the next major encounter and established a new form of sea battle, where the opposing fleets never came in sight of each other, all fighting being done by aircraft. Good intelligence gave the Americans the chance to 'bounce' their opponent's carriers with their decks full of refuelling aircraft. The Japanese lost four carriers as against one American.

Their operations now had to be conducted at a reduced level and they were finally beaten in 1944 during the battles of the so-called 'Marianas Turkey Shoot'. Here the Japanese lost three more carriers and, more seriously, the bulk of their remaining trained aircrew. So few remained that the remnants of the once-proud carrier force were used as a suicide decoy a few months later at Leyte Gulf.

Few large Japanese carriers were completed during the war. One

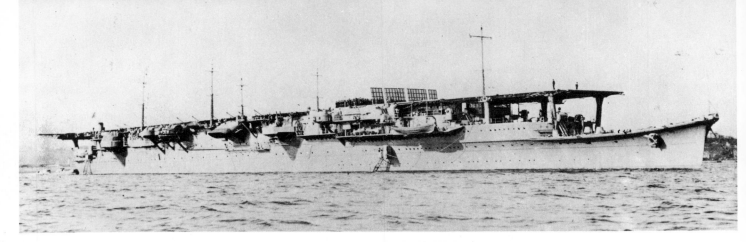

above
The Japanese carrier *Shoho*, shown on completion of her conversion from an auxiliary vessel. She was sunk soon after at the Coral Sea action. Note the island-less, hangar-on-top construction, with down-turned funnel casing.

left
The American carrier *Wasp* burns off Guadalcanal after being torpedoed by a Japanese submarine.

left, below
Aftermath of a Kamikaze strike on the American escort carrier *Belleau Wood*. Note the wooden flight-deck, which offered little protection.

opposite
Activity aboard the American attack carrier *Shangri La*, a modernised Essex-class unit.

was *Taiho*, lost off the Marianas; another was the enormous *Shinano*, built from the third Musashi battle-ship hull but torpedoed and sunk before entering service. They attempted series production with the Unryu class but had little success, due to long lead times. The Allies also discovered that large, quality ships could not easily be produced quickly under wartime conditions. Even the Americans' great capacity enabled them to concentrate only on the Essex class. Being built at the same time were the three armour-decked Mid-ways of 45,000 tons, but these were not completed in time for action.

The British tried to cut a corner by constructing the *Colossus* and *Majestic* class of 'Light Fleet Carrier' to civilian standards under Lloyds Register classification, but those completed were also too late for action. The same applied to the following Albions, although all proved useful for subsequent peace-time uses. Over-ambitiously the four 37,000-ton Audacious and

three 45,000-ton Gibraltars were also laid down but without a hope of being completed in time. Long after the war, just two of the former were finished, as *Ark Royal* and *Eagle*.

By the close of hostilities, the carrier was firmly established as the new capital ship, with a flexibility and striking power far exceeding that of any battleship. Destruction by aircraft of both *Tirpitz* and the remaining Japanese heavy units underlined the end of the rule of the big gun.

With so much war-built tonnage available, the Americans and British built no more carriers for some years, but the latter came up with several important developments. The steam catapult enabled heavy aircraft to be operated from smaller flightdecks; angled decks made simultaneous landings and take-offs possible, made better use of flightdeck area and enabled overshoots to come round for another approach; the mirror landing aid gave the pilot optical information on the correctness of his approach. With the introduction at sea of jet aircraft which have poor low-speed characteristics, the Americans capitalised on these innovations, incorporating them all in the new Forrestals of the early 1950s. Where the Midways had seemed large at 45,000 tons, these new ships were of 60,000. Their length of nearly 1,040 feet was on a par with the great liner *Queen Elizabeth* and they were unable to go through the Panama Canal.

Before the Forrestal programme was completed, the revolutionary *Enterprise* introduced the nuclear carrier. Her 75,000 tons could be propelled almost indefinitely by steam drawn from boilers heated by eight reactors. With no uptakes or funnel the island was much smaller and point defence was by missile rather than by gun.

Britain's economy could not cope with the spiralling costs of carriers and no new conventional ones were built, those scrapped not being replaced. Even the Americans have probably reached the ultimate in the 92,000-ton Nimitz class. The third, and probably the last, of these will cost over

1,000,000,000 dollars but can operate over 100 large aircraft and has a crew of over 6,000. Their value, and the threat that they pose, means that their every movement is likely to be monitored by satellite and they will be individually targeted by waiting missiles. It seems that the pure strike carrier concept may now be defeated by its size and cost.

Many navies, however, do not need full strike facilities and, re-appraisals are being made utilising helicopters and STOL aircraft, neither of which need vast flightdecks. Thus we have two main developments, the helicopter carrier and the helicopter cruiser. The first is typified by the American Iwo Jimas, which look like aircraft carriers but lack catapults and arrestor gear, and use a mixed bag of helicopters for either anti-submarine or assault work. The second was really started by the hybrid French *Jeanne d'Arc*, continued by the Italians and then by the Russian Moskvas. As part of the new Soviet 'blue water' navy the task of the Moskvas is primarily to destroy ICBM-carrying submarines and they have little offensive power apart from helicopters and SAM's.

The world's first nuclear-propelled carrier, the U.S.S. *Enterprise*. Note the small, funnel-less island, fixed 'billboard' radar antenna, the wide variety of aircraft, side elevators and surface-to-air missiles.

opposite
The American Iwo Jima-class assault ships were designed to operate helicopters in the assault or A/S modes. A CH-46 Sea Knight is here seen leaving on a sortie during the Vietnam war.

Both these French and Russian types have superstructures blocking the flightdeck and can operate the new STOL aircraft only in a VTOL role. As the latter's performance is greatly increased by a short take-off run, we see the Moskva class abandoned after the first two and superseded by the larger KIEVs, with an angled deck. At up to 40,000 tons and also armed offensively with SSMs, this type of ship may be a reason for America to build yet more strike carriers. In concept and general layout, however, they are enlarged versions of the Invincible class now under construction in Britain. To obtain maximum use of flight deck length the forward end may be angled up slightly in a 'ski-jump' to assist STOL aircraft, such as the Harrier, into the air, saving fuel and increasing payload.

Submarines

the silent scourge

Ezra Lee's unsuccessful attempt to sink H.M.S. *Eagle* in 1776 was the first offensive use of a submerged vehicle but their ancestry predates this by at least 150 years, for the Dutchman Cornelius Drebbel built a submersible in 1620. The idea of the submarine inspired inventors, and by the end of the nineteenth century technology was beginning to catch up with their ideas.

Thus in 1879 the optimistically-named *Resurgam* was built by an English priest named Garrett. It incorporated ballast tanks with which it trimmed to neutral buoyancy and then relied on water flow over hydroplanes to drive it under. In military terms these advanced ideas were rather offset by its dependence on a steam engine and lack of armament (due perhaps to its clerical origins).

Garrett may well have been influenced by the earlier *Ictineo* of the Spaniard Monturiol or *Le Plongeur* of the Frenchmen Brun and Bougois. Both these used compressed air for blowing tanks. The great Swedish inventor Nordenfeldt incorporated the best current ideas in his boat of 1885. It had a steam engine and vertical propellers to drive it under, and its revolutionary feature was a launching tube for a Whitehead torpedo. This marriage of craft and weapon was indeed prophetic.

The Spaniard Peral shortly afterward built the first boat to be driven submerged by an electric motor. This saved precious air but was of low endurance because of the primitive batteries then available. In the same year, 1888, the French-built *Gymnote* re-introduced the hydroplane on a 60-foot,

A German U-boat of the First World War under fire and preparing to dive. Most submarines of this era attacked on the surface and were then at their most vulnerable.

cigar-shaped hull. This craft provided the experience for the construction of the *Gustave Zédé* of 1893, which was a really practical 150-footer which carried out successful torpedo attacks in exercises against surface ships. The French Navy, ever mindful of a weapon to up-end Britain's maritime superiority, were sufficiently impressed to employ the engineer Laubeuf to build the *Narval* of 1899. This was very advanced in having ballast tanks external to a strong pressure hull, and also a petrol engine for surface running. This also drove a charging set for the batteries which powered an electric motor when submerged.

Officially dismissed in Britain as 'weapons of a weaker power', submarines were being viewed seriously by men of vision. For in America, too, one was being built for the navy in 1895, the fruit of 20

years development by a man called Holland. Soon afterwards the Admiralty purchased one of his petrol-driven craft for evaluation and followed this by a further five at the end of 1901. They were only 63 feet in length and were plagued internally by petrol fumes, a problem solved by the French by using the newly-invented diesel engine. One improvement that the British made to their Hollands was to install a periscope.

They were immediately followed by 13 A-class boats. These were over 100 feet in length and one was experimentally diesel-propelled. Still incredibly primitive, they were proved, mainly by the

top
A Holland-class submarine, probably
No. 1, alongside her parent ship, the
ex-torpedo-gunboat *Hazard*.

above
The German U-36 was completed in
1914 and sunk by a Q-ship during the
following year. The light W/T masts
were collapsible.

dedication and enthusiasm of their
crews, to be a real danger to surface
ships. Eleven 'B's and 38 'C's were
built by 1907 and attested to their
Lordships' change of mind. Not
until 1910, in the 'D' class, was the
diesel universally adopted for surface running. A conning tower of
substantial size and a hull casing
were now features, together with
two 18-inch torpedo tubes forward
and one aft. In addition, the ballast
tanks were sited externally on the
hull, introducing the so-called
'saddle-tank' design.

The mainstay of Britain's submarine fleet in the First World War
was the 'E' class, of which there
were 55. They were of 800 tons
submerged, on a hull length of 180
feet, were equipped with wireless,
a gun and five 18-inch torpedo
tubes, two forward one aft and two
firing on the beam. They could
make 16 knots on the surface and
10 submerged.

The Germans were late constructing submarines, the 280-ton
U-1 being completed in 1906 by
the Germaniawerft, a name later
synonymous with the type. The
team proved to be most excellent
designers, gaining experience
greatly from export orders. Boats

followed each other in small groups, each an improvement on the last in both size and armament. Design reached something of a plateau from U-19 onwards, with a length of about 210 feet and a submerged tonnage of 840. They carried a heavier gun than their British equivalents and four 19.7-inch torpedo tubes.

At the outbreak of war, Germany had about 30 boats to Britain's 70. They were to be used in different ways but neither side could produce an effective counter to the other. Once submerged submarines could be detected only by the crude hydrophone, and were vulnerable only to moored nets and mines.

Britain used them imaginatively in the Dardanelles campaign, but the U-boats struck back effectively when they arrived. The Fleet was forced to give up its traditional close-support role and operate from a secure base. Germany rapidly realised that, where they were not strong enough to oppose the Royal Navy by conventional methods, the U-boat would enable them to take the offensive. All had guns mounted and sank more merchantmen by this means than by torpedoes. In addition, the UB classes were built for inshore work and the UC classes for minelaying. The

standard sea-going types were augmented after 1917 by boats of up to nearly 2,800 tons submerged, designed to take the war across the Atlantic. America had come in mainly because of the unrestricted use of the submarine against shipping.

By 1917, the losses to British merchant ships were approaching crisis point. The answer was found in the convoy. By proceeding in company, ships were closely grouped and were harder to find

and the submarines had to come in to attack, giving the escorts a chance to hit back. Losses dropped dramatically. The war never produced an effective anti-submarine weapon, however, and desperation demanded such ventures as the attempted blocking of Zeebrugge and Ostend to deny the U-boats their bases.

Early on, the British attempted to counter submarine with submarine. The little 'R' class boats

top
Completed in 1910, the British C-class submarine C34 displaced 320 tons submerged. She was torpedoed off the Shetlands in 1917 by the German U52.

above
The British B10 of 1906 displays to advantage the clean lines typical of many early submarines.

British E-class submarine during the Dardanelles operations of the First World War. The Es were the first really effective patrol submarines built for the Royal Navy.

of 1918 were streamlined, single-screwed and filled mostly with batteries to give a submerged speed of 15 knots. They had six bow tubes for torpedoes but their sensors did not measure up to the conception of tracking prey through their use. Where the German U-boat had a clearly defined objective, to sink Allied ships, the British equivalent was faced with a sea largely clear of the enemy and its role was not so obvious, resulting in an over-abundance of suggestions. One of these was for a Fleet Submarine, large and fast enough to accompany the main body of the fleet at 24 knots. These were produced as the 'K' class, steam turbine-propelled because no diesels were powerful enough. They had three

guns and two funnels, which had to be blanked-off before diving. They proved disappointing in service and incredibly prone to both collision and accident.

The last four hulls of the type were rebuilt as the diesel-driven 'M' class. They mounted an old 12-inch gun which could elevate to some degree, but not train. It could be fired from an awash position but the submarine had to surface to reload so there was little advantage in this. M.2 was later rebuilt with a seaplane and catapult and M.3 converted into a minelayer.

The 'big submarine' idea persisted, producing the 3,600-ton X1 in 1923. With four 5.2-inch guns in twin mountings, she was designed to operate on the surface against 'soft' targets. Of far more significance however was the improvement in the standard patrol submarine with the extended 'L' class being developed from the successful E's. The class was 36

strong, with a submerged displacement topping 1,000 tons, and the last group of them having 21-inch torpedoes against the earlier 18-inch.

The trend to larger boats continued the 'O', 'P' and 'R' classes, capable of 18 knots on the surface and armed with eight torpedoes tubes and a 4-inch gun. Like the many contemporary Italian boats, however, they proved excellent for peacetime uses but too large for war, where their lack of handiness was responsible for many losses.

Those usually rational submarine designers, the French, also produced an aberration in the incredible *Surcouf*. At nearly 3,000 tons on the surface, she disposed of two 8-inch guns and a spotter seaplane.

With the America–Japan rivalry increasing its momentum, both navies built large submarine fleets. The problems of the vast distances posed by the Pacific tended to

left
The deep water below the Arctic ice cap is a safe haven for the nuclear submarine, which can operate undetected and surface in one of the many thin-ice areas. Here, H.M.S. *Dreadnought* is seen at the North Pole.

below
The old fleet base at Singapore now sees little of the Royal Navy. The nuclear attack submarine is well capable of travelling there submerged.

opposite, top
The complexity of a modern submarine is well illustrated by this picture of the control room of the British Polaris submarine *Resolution*.

opposite, lower
The four nuclear-powered submarines of the Resolution class carry the Polaris missiles of Britain's strategic deterrent, Here, *Renown* slips under the Forth Bridge.

right
Seen here in Scottish waters during the
Second World War, the French
submarine *Surcouf* typified the 'cruiser
submarine' concept. Launched in 1929,
she was armed with two 8-inch guns
and carried a seaplane.

below, right
Eighteen mines could be laid by the
German UCII submarines of 1916. The
increased freeboard of the forward
casing improved seakeeping.

above
British submarine E31 in dry-dock,
showing the elaborate guards designed
to prevent nets entangling the after
hydroplanes.

opposite
Completed after the First World War,
the Japanese I-51 was an early example
of their fleet submarines. Note the large
size and cluttered appearance.

produce large ships, and submarines followed the trend with
the Japanese, as ever, being
obsessed with size.

With the introduction of ASDIC
(later SONAR) and effective depth
charges in the '20s, surface escorts
could at last take on a submerged
submarine with a good chance of
success, and the smaller and more
handy boats were the ones most
likely to survive an attack. Significantly, when the Germans again
started submarine construction in
the 1930s, it was the smaller type
of boat that they built. The British
wisely concentrated on only two
classes, the 60-plus 'S' class of
medium range, and the long range
'T's which numbered about 50.
Even the 'S' class proved a little
large for inshore and Mediterranean
work, so the little 'U' class, designed

as a practice submarine, went into
series production. With four tubes,
it was developed into the 'V' type.

The largest submarine force
at the outbreak of the Second
World War was that of the enig-
matic Russian fleet. Consisting of
between 150 and 170 boats, it
achieved very little. The Germans
started with a surprisingly small
but highly professional force. They
concentrated on the Typ VIIc
general-purpose boat and the larger
Typ IX. With the British immediately instituting the convoy system
which had saved them in the earlier
war, it was obvious that Donitz'
U-boat force had anticipated it and
organised itself well.

Again mercantile sinkings were
by gun rather than torpedo, with
submarines boldly surfacing in the
middle of convoys at night, the

escort's early ASDIC often being blanketed by so many ships. 'Wolf-pack' tactics were also very effective with a sighting submarine or long range aircraft, such as the FW 200 Kondor, homing all available boats in for a combined attack, swamping the escorts.

Radar proved a powerful weapon for the Allies. Escorts could now 'see' U-boats moving in to a night attack on the surface and airborne patrols with radar, searchlights and depthcharges made life very difficult for submarines on passage to and from their patrol areas. Proceeding submerged was a slow process and surfacing, which was still necessary, for recharging batteries, became gradually almost suicidal. One remedy was a powerful battery of A/A weapons in the submarine, but salvation lay in the development of a Dutch idea, the Schnorkel or Snort mast, which enabled a submarine to run on

diesels whilst submerged and recharge at the same time.

The surface escorts were gaining strength in both effectiveness and numbers. Where the U-boats had tended to ignore them when stalking their charges, they could no longer do so, and employed the acoustic torpedo, which homed on to the escort's higher-revving propellers. However, improved weapons were being used by the specialist A/S frigates, the Hedge-hog and the later Squid firing ahead of a ship on to a submerged target still firmly in the ASDIC beam.

But it was the aircraft which beat the U-boat finally, hounding it ceaselessly from both shore bases and escort carriers. For a submarine to surface was to court disaster and the Germans actively pursued the true submarine design, stream-lined, fast and able to stay submerged indefinitely. The Typ

XXI and Typ XXIII were coming into production at the war's end but arrived too late. Promising experiments were being conducted on the Walther hydrogen peroxide-driven turbine, a closed-circuit system that needed no air. Postwar experience showed it to be unstable, however, and it was abandoned.

The Japanese war effort was largely destroyed by American submarines which operated, like the Germans, against a large merchant fleet but with the advantage that Japanese defence was poorly organised. The large Japanese submarine force was comparatively unsuccessful in its efforts against an enemy with vastly superior technology and capacity. Their large submarines included the I-400 class, which displaced over 6,000 tons submerged and which each operated three seaplanes. Aircraft from one of these were the only

opposite, top
The little Type 205s were West Germany's first post-war submarines. They were highly manoeuvrable and carried a battery of eight torpedo tubes forward, but suffered from troubles with the steel used for the hull.

opposite, lower
The powerful AA armament of these U-boats and the thickness of their Trondheim bunkers testify to the threat posed by aircraft.

right
Air power was the key to the defeat of the U-boat in the Atlantic during the Second World War, to the point where even routine surfacing or 'snorting' to recharge batteries became suicidal. This example fell victim to both depth-charging and strafing from an Australian Sunderland flying boat.

ones to bomb the U.S. mainland during the whole war.

Postwar developments of the submarine aimed at increasing battery capacity and streamlining for higher submerged speeds. Guns were removed and conning towers, or fins, heightened to encompass the earlier periscope standards. Then, in 1954, the U.S. Navy commissioned the *Nautilus*, the first nuclear submarine. Capable of operating submerged at high speed for an indefinite period, she had the legs of any weather-dominated escort. She was the beginning of a warship revolution more profound than that caused by the Dreadnought. The new capital ship had been born.

As with all major precedents, the main rival navies were quick to follow. Russia and Britain, began with fleet submarines, or hunter/killers as they were sometimes called. A new, and more sinister, phase began in 1959, when the *George Washington* was commissioned as the first Polaris submarine. Carrying 16 missiles, she began the transfer of the nation's nuclear deterrent from the Strategic Air Command and triggered the explosive growth of the Soviet Navy to counter it. The latest class deploys the MIRV-headed Trident

missile with a range of over 4,000 miles, which required the Soviet Navy to build ships capable of operating world-wide.

As no sea escort vessel can hope to out-distance a submerged nuclear submarine, the helicopter has been rapidly developed as a counter. Targets can be detected by sensors on the sea bed or dropped from the air. They can be destroyed by a homing torpedo dropped from a helicopter or from a long range carrier such as ASROC, which can also deliver a nuclear-headed depth charge. A promising new weapon is

CAPTOR, or captive torpedo, an encapsulated 'homer' sown on the sea bed, lying dormant until triggered by an enemy submarine's 'noise signature'. Submarine can destroy submarine by SUBROC missile, a surface target by an encapsulated SSM or a helicopter by a small missile such as the British SLAAM.

The fleet submarine is still deployed only by America, Britain and Russia. In addition to attack duties, they act increasingly as escorts to important Task Groups.

ICBM submarines carry the main strategic deterrents of not only the

The U.S.S. *Nautilus* was the world's first nuclear submarine. Completed in 1954, she heralded the arrival of a new era in warship technology, although still armed with conventional weapons.

above powers but also those of France. They seek to avoid detection and will not go into action except in self-defence. In addition, there is still a place for the conventional patrol submarines, which have the advantage of extreme quietness. Good modern examples include the British 'O' class, the French Daphnes and the German Type 206.

Finally, brief mention should be made of the midget submarine. These have been over-glamourised in postwar years for the numerous types produced by the German and Japanese navies achieved little. The British 35-ton X-craft were little more successful in general but justified their existence by the crippling of the German battleship *Tirpitz*. They were not armed with torpedoes but with large charges which could be dropped beneath a target. Frogmen were also used to attach charges directly. The Italians also used this method effectively, although they used a modified torpedo as a carrier rather than a true submarine.

The Cruiser

With a more homogeneous armament of 6-inch guns in the Diadems of 1897 and the Monmouths of 1901, the British began to develop the cruiser away from the 'cut-down battleship' approach which had dominated the class. The big armoured cruisers were still built, up to the Minotaurs of 1906. Although direct descendants of the Powerfuls, they had less freeboard and top hamper and a mixed armament of four 9.2-inch and 10 7.5-inch guns, an arrangement about to be superseded by the new battle cruiser concept. Although of 14,600 tons they would have been outclassed in a fight by the ultimate German design, the pair of Scharnhorsts. Of only 11,400 tons, these nevertheless disposed of eight 8.2-inch and six 5.9s, like the preceding Roons. Both types of gun were exceedingly effective and mounted high enough to use in a seaway. British practice put too much of the secondary armament low down in casemates.

Other notable equivalents were the French *Edgar Quinet*, with a

The battle cruiser was designed to counter the large armoured cruiser, a task that it performed superlatively well at the Falklands when the *Scharnhorst* and *Gneisenau* were despatched after a gallant fight.

single calibre armament of 14 7.6-inch guns and the American Tennessees with no less than four 10-inch and 16 6-inch weapons, and imposing enough to share the State names normally reserved for battleships.

The British 6-inch ships referred to above were 'protected' cruisers but in 1905 a new type called a 'Scout' was introduced and began the line of light cruisers which carried their armament on a high-speed and largely unarmoured hull.

The pair of 2,900-ton Sentinels were the first and designed to act as flotilla leaders to the larger destroyers. Their armament was only of 4-inch calibre, which persisted through the classes until the 1912 Actives. They were paralleled by a

right
The mixed 9.2- and 6-inch armament of the pre-Dreadnought protected cruisers is typified by the British Drakes of 1901. Shown here is the *Good Hope*, Cradock's flagship at Coronel in 1914, where she was totally out-classed and sunk with all hands.

below
The British Arethusas of 1913–14 had much of the dash of the destroyers with which they cooperated. The nameship, shown, was lost to a mine off Felixstowe in 1916. Note the mixed 4- and 6-inch armament.

bottom
The German light cruiser *Emden* showed once again, in 1914, how difficult it is to bring a determinedly-handled commerce raider to book. She tied down large Allied forces in the Indian Ocean before being destroyed by the Australian cruiser *Sydney*.

series of German light cruisers with 4.1-inch guns but with tonnages that slowly increased to 5,500 in the Karlsruhes.

With destroyers now becoming larger, the 'destroyer-leader' role was being taken over by purpose-built ships. The Scouts were stretched, with the Bristols, to take a brace of 6-inch guns to supplement their 4-inch ones and it was but a short step thence to the all 6-inch armament in the Weymouths and succeeding classes, all of which had four funnels and superb, lean looks. Their moderate speeds tied them to fleet work. The little 3,500-ton *Arethusas* of 1914 reversed the trend to mixed armament but could make 29 knots on greatly increased power and again worked mainly in conjunction with destroyers. They led the way to the long line of the successful 'C' class which reintroduced a homogeneous 6-inch battery. The first group of 'C's had three funnels but succeeding groups had only two after a machinery rearrangement in which the geared turbine was adopted, reducing propeller speeds.

The German cruisers adopted the 5.9-inch gun so that the British had no advantage, and the light cruiser types were remarkably well matched.

At the beginning of the First World War, the Germans had commerce raiders, regular and auxiliary, strategically placed to fall upon merchant shipping. Cruisers were used extensively and independently to track them down. Older units were employed on blockade duties.

The large armoured cruiser had been effectively outmoded by the battle cruiser, a lesson underlined by von Spee's defeat at the Falklands and later by the British losses at Jutland, which effectively spelt the end of the type, the survivors being used largely as convoy escorts.

The smaller cruisers, fast and compact, had a multitude of uses and the 'C's developed into 'D's and 'E's, gradually increasing in size and armament but keeping to the single, open 6-inch mountings. Another feature was the large number of torpedo tubes carried, although these never seemed to be treated as a prime weapon in British practice, probably due to their earlier lack of success with the specialist torpedo cruiser. Abroad however, the torpedo was regarded differently, particularly by the Japanese. Their little 3,600-ton

above
Ceremonial plays a major rôle in the peacetime routine of every navy. Here Dutch sailors 'man ship' in front of a cruiser's 57mm gunhouse.

left
In February 1942 a powerful German squadron broke up the English Channel from Brest to Wilhelmshaven. This German photograph purports to show the heavy cruiser *Prinz Eugen* firing on Dover during the operation – but the fact that she is firing to starboard makes this rather doubtful!

right
Overaged warships can perform valuable
service by undertaking assignments in
less demanding operations and leaving
more modern units free to be deployed
in major combat areas. Thus the French
cruiser *Bruix* was active at Salonika and
the Dardanelles and, later, during the
protracted Cameroons operation.

above
A typical lot of the cruiser was convoy
escort. This photograph shows the
forward 5.25-inch turret of a British
Dido-class ship, trained on an after
bearing to minimise water problems
during heavy weather on the Russian
route.

above, right
The American New Orleans-class of
8-inch-gunned cruisers were laid down
as far back as 1931, but provided a
design sound enough to form the basis
of those classes built during the War
Emergency programmes. One feature
not carried over, however, was the
disproportionately large after superstructure, containing hangar space for
no less than four aircraft.

Tatsatus, for instance, could make
33 knots and pose a real threat, and
they went on eventually to develop
the type into the formidable Kita-
kamis.

By the end of the war, cruiser
sizes were rapidly increasing with,
for instance, the four-funnelled
protected Omaha's of the U.S.
Navy being soon exceeded by the
British Effinghams. These ships,
looking like overgrown 'C's, were
of 10,000 tons and the largest of
their type, being built on the
strength of a (false) rumour that
the Germans were building a class
of super-cruiser. They were armed
with single, hand-worked 7.5-inch
guns which fired projectiles heavy
enough to tax the strength of the
strongest loading number. The
class had a great influence on future
cruiser design because their existence caused the Washington Treaty
limits to be set at 10,000 tons, with
guns not exceeding 8-inch. Britain
was thus inadvertently a cause of
escalation, as these limits rapidly

came to be taken as the norm.

The Japanese, particularly, produced a whole series of excellent
cruisers, their designers tending
not to take the tonnage limits too
seriously. Thus the Nachi and
Atago classes of 1924–8 carried 10
8-inch guns and were protected
well enough to weigh-in at nearly
13,000 tons. They were followed
by the Mogami and Tone groups,
the latter carrying five triple 6-inch
turrets and leading to the American
reply of the near-identical Brooklyns. The Japanese ships were fast
and armed with up to 12 torpedo
tubes, firing the 24-inch Long
Lance torpedo, to be used with
deadly effect at the Java Sea action
in 1942.

By keeping to the treaty limitations the American cruisers made
do with nine 8-inch guns in the
Northampton and New Orleans
classes, the last of which, *Wichita*,
differed and formed a virtual prototype for all U.S. Navy heavy
cruisers for the next decade.

116

top

Responding to the stimulus of the fast ships produced by the neighbouring Italians, the French proved adept at building cruisers of excellent performance. The *Gloire* of 1935 was one of six carrying nine 6-inch guns, and is shown in a typical Second World War colour scheme.

centre

The handsome German heavy cruiser *Prinz Eugen* was the only completed unit of the three projected Lützow class, themselves enlarged Hippers. She survived the *Bismarck* operation, the up-Channel dash in 1942, and the A-bomb at Bikini. She finally succumbed to another American nuclear explosion at Kwajalein in 1947.

lower

The American's success in the rapid expansion of their fleet during the Second World War was due in no small measure to the series production of a few basic designs. Thus, the *Vincennes* belonged to the Cleveland class of light cruisers of which no less than 27 were completed. Note the very symmetrical layout and the high freeboard aft to accommodate the hangar for the two Kingfisher float planes.

Having started the heavy cruiser competition, Britain produced the majestic three-funnelled County class, and two smaller derivatives, in the 1920s. With liner-like freeboard and machinery for 32 knots, they had little allowance left for protection. With these completed, the Royal Navy abandoned the 8-inch cruiser for the smaller cheaper and more versatile 6-inch ship, reintroduced with the five Leanders. Although the immediate successors to these were kept to a modest size, continuing large foreign designs, particularly French and Japanese, resulted in the Southamptons, with four triple 6-inch mountings on a tonnage of about 9,000. They were followed by the more austere Crown Colony class, which, with small variations, was the final conventional British design.

Increasing threat from aircraft prior to the Second World War resulted in some of the veteran C-class being rearmed with high-angle 4-inch guns and a new class, the elegant Didos, with 5.25-inch guns. The Americans built the broadly similar 5-inch-armed Atlanta class, both groups having an extremely active war.

The French and Italian navies tended to build in direct competition but, where the latter designed for speed and armament at the expense of endurance and protection, the French produced well-balanced cruisers of which the *Algérie* was a good example. The corresponding Italian class was the Bolzanos; fine ships in their way, but exceeding treaty limits.

In the late 1930s the Italians build the splendidly-named Capitani Romani class. These interesting little 3,500-ton cruisers disposed of 120,000 shp for a speed of nearly 40 knots. Although classed as cruisers, they were matched for size, and outgunned, by the large French Mogador-class destroyers.

The German *Emden* of 1925 commenced a series of sound little 5.9-inch-gunned cruisers, embodying welded construction to save weight. The Karlsruhes were interesting in having one triple turret forward and two aft, the latter staggered to improve ammunition handling. The 8-inch Hipper class was not built until after the treaty had been largely abandoned.

The *Deutschland* of 1929 was an example of what could be packed into a modest-sized hull (even though it was of about 12,000 tons). She was the first of three armoured cruisers, so formidably armed that they were universally termed 'pocket battleships'. They carried two triple 11-inch guns, eight single 5.9's and three twin 4.1's, together with torpedo tubes and a spotter aircraft. Commerce raiding was their prime function and eight diesels coupled to two shafts conferred long range and ease of maintenance. They also began a trend to bulbous bows in large German warships. Although the design was highly individual, it did

left
The handsome Italian destroyer *Andrea Doria* includes four light A/S helicopters in her armament. She has an American Terrier SAM launcher forward and four 76mm guns on either beam.

below
The Italian light cruiser *San Marco* started life as one of the Capitani Romani class, which originally were capable of some 39 knots on no less than 110,000 shp.

opposite, top
Among the last of the Royal Navy's conventional cruisers, *Tiger* and *Blake* were expensively rebuilt aft to operate an A/S flight of four Sea King helicopters.

not move any major navy to direct reply.

Only America produced cruisers in any numbers during the Second World War, standardising on two basic designs, incorporating either 12 6-inch or nine 8-inch guns. The war saw cruisers employed in the usual wide variety of roles. They were very effectively used in groups, such as by the Japanese at the Java Sea and the British at the River Plate or against the *Scharnhorst*. They were used in the classic 'track and report' role during the *Bismarck* incident, and both sides found them effective against commerce. The Americans used them greatly as screens for Task Groups, but, above all, they fought the convoys through, particularly to Malta and Russia, against surface attack. The Second Battle of Sirte was a model of this kind of action.

The ultimate expression of the cruiser was the trio of Des Moines. Still extant, they each displace more than the 1906 *Dreadnought*, with turbines generating six times her power. With their mixed armament of eight, five and three-inch calibres, however, the wheel had turned once again and a new rationalisation was required. This was triggered by the introduction of the guided missile. These had already been used during the war: the Germans used air-launched, radio-controlled glider bombs with notable success at Anzio and in the sinking of the surrendered Italian

battleship *Roma*; the Japanese preferred the Kamikaze, the guidance system here being a human pilot.

The first outward result produced by the latter was the trading by the Americans of the vast number of 20 and 40-millimetre weapons that festooned their ships for the 3-inch, firing proximity-fused ammunition. The stopping power of even these was insufficient in all cases, however; what was needed was a weapon capable of distintegrating an incoming aircraft. A carrier could use her own aircraft but a surface-to-air guided missile (or SAM) was required by other classes of ship. The Americans had the Terrier flying by the end of the 1940s and at sea in cruiser conversions by 1955.

The longer-ranged Talos soon followed, with a nuclear warhead capability. Only the small-scale *Albany* and *Galveston* conversions were attempted as the fine, subdivided hulls did not lend themselves easily to their new role. Their rebuilding proved prolonged, expensive and less than perfect; a few other navies attempted it, the British not at all. Obviously capacious purpose-built ships were required.

The conventional cruiser began to slip into genteel obsolescence – except for one last, peculiar twitch. The Russians, chagrined at their fleet's nondescript performance in the war, began constructing ambitiously in the 1950s. They produced the extended class of 16,000-

ton Sverdlovs which were obsolete on completion, but would have made formidable commerce raiders. They were a straight development of the prewar Kirov and Chapaev classes and their 5.9-inch armament and director systems were a throwback to the days of cooperation with German designers prior to 1941.

Except for the Russians, no first-line fleet now operates conventional gun-armed cruisers and the title has become meaningless except as an indication of size. Purpose-built gun/missile hybrids have grown from overgrown destroyers such as the British Countys, American Leahys and Russian Kyndas to such formidable units as the Virginias and Russian Karas. There is now a common factor in that both of the latter are geared to the defence of task groups, a comparatively recent departure for the Soviet navy.

Another line of development has been the so-called 'Helicopter Cruiser'. The starting-point here was the French *Jeanne d'Arc* of 1964 – a cruiser forward with a flight-deck aft – although the basic layout had been followed over 30 years before by the Japanese in the conversions of the *Ise* and *Hyuga* battleships. On a standard tonnage of about 10,000 the French design can operate eight large helicopters; the rest of her armament is primarily anti-ship, with guns and six Exocet SSMs (surface-to-surface missiles).

centre
The fifteen 6-inch guns of the Japanese Mogami class cruisers were the stimulus for the American Brooklyns. Being of greater tonnage than Treaty limits agreed, they were later easily converted by exchanging their triple gun-houses for twin 8-inch. *Mogami* herself, shown here, barely survived a severe mauling at Midway and was finally sunk at Leyte Gulf in 1944.

right
The Russian Sverdlovs made a great impression on their first appearances in the West. As conventionally-armed cruisers, however, they were obsolescent even on completion. *Ordzhonikidze* is here shown on a state visit to the U.K. Note the mine-laying rails on the after deck.

The Italians have built two classes on the same principles, with helicopter flights and Terrier SAM systems. More recently the Japanese have built the Harunas and plan a larger design.

The Royal Navy's contribution to the type has been the expensive rebuilding of two Tiger-class cruisers, which look all wrong and whose capacity of four Sea King helicopters hardly seems good value. It can fairly be said, however, that the type is firmly established although American and later British thinking tends towards carrier type vessels with more amphibious attack capacity.

The Russians extended the idea to the two 15,000-ton Moskvas which, with about 15 helicopters and a long range anti-submarine missile launcher, can carry out A/S operations over an extended period. They carry also a heavy SAM and torpedo armament. That only two were built may well be due to the fact that their design does not lend itself to STOL operation and the angled-deck Kievs would be a logical step, similar to that of the British progress from the Tigers to the *Invincible* 'through-deck cruiser'.

above
A most formidable antagonist, the Russian *Kara* was developed from the *Kresta II*. She repeated weapon systems and added even more. Alongside the large funnel casing (probably denoting gas turbine propulsion) can be seen the lidded silo of the fast-reaction SA-N-4 close-range systems.

The small Dutch cruiser *Jacob van Heemskerck* differed from her near-sister *Tromp* by being completed in a British yard with a light 4-inch armament. Both served with distinction during the Second World War.

left
To operate in a nuclear fall-out zone without precaution would mean contaminated top surfaces. Warships are therefore fitted with a 'pre-wetting' system, shown here on an American Worcester-class light cruiser.

The Destroyer

The early TBDs tended to have failings arising largely from their size. In British designs no less than seven kinds of water-tube boilers were used and the scantlings were not up to extended operation in a seaway. Everything aboard was permanently wet as any sort of sea washed over them. They had turtle-backs to shed water quickly, but even so life aboard was far from healthy. German practice from 1899 had been to design with a raised forecastle, and these ships were so obviously drier that the British adopted it in the Rivers of 1903. Having built 36 of these the Admiralty followed with the Tribals, whose turbine propulsion hefted their speed to over 33 knots. The later group were of over 1,000 tons and introduced the 4-inch gun.

In contrast, the German contemporaries were of only about 700 tons and much closer to the torpedo boat concept. They were all numbered rather than named, often carrying trainable torpedo tubes in a well between the raised forecastle and the bridge.

As a variation on the 'cruiser-leader' the British built the outsize *Swift* in 1907. Her 2,200 tons were not eclipsed in the Royal Navy until the Battle class appeared in 1945, and she had the speed to keep up with her charges. For her size, she was lightly armed with four 4-inch guns, but later sported a single 6-inch forward. She was not repeated or even equalled for size until the Germans built the 2,300-ton leaders S113 and V116 in 1918. On paper these were formidable ships, with four 5.9-inch guns and four large torpedo tubes, but they proved to be slow and indifferent.

above
The first turbine-driven destroyer was H.M.S. *Viper*, which achieved a dramatic improvement in speed over the earlier 'up-and-downers'. This 1899 trials picture shows her at over $36\frac{1}{2}$ knots. Note the 'squat' by the stern.

below
The French destroyer *Boutefele* was a typical European design of about 1907/8.

At the outbreak of war the Admiralty took over two groups of large destroyers building in the U.K. for Chile and Turkey. These were commissioned as the Botha and Talisman-class leaders, complementing the purpose-built Marksman class. Destroyer flotillas ranged between 10 to well over 20 boats and classes were large (e.g. the Admiralty M's were 85 strong) and the leader was an essential part of their control. Before the end of the war the Shakespeare and Bruce classes were completed but, from the V and W's onward, it was customary to build in smaller groups of eight, with one extra fitted as leader.

Large numbers of two- and three-funnelled destroyers formed the basis of the Grand Fleet flotillas, the 'L', 'M', 'R' and 'S' groups each being improvements on those preceding. All were of between 1,000 and 1,100-ton raised-

forecastle design and capable of 33–36 knots. Their armament was also standard at three 4-inch guns and four torpedo tubes.

This general specification covered also the majority of German destroyers, except that they normally had six tubes. As early as 1915 they, too, were building small numbers of boats to match the British leaders, with an extra gun and machinery of up to 42,000 shp. This order of power could be generated in small hulls only by virtue of the compactness of steam turbine machinery. Prior to the 'L' class, these had been directly coupled to propellers, which revolved inefficiently at very high speeds. In 1914 single reduction gearing was introduced, bringing shaft speeds down to more acceptable levels. All destroyers were, in addition, oil burners, this system having been first introduced in the British Tribals.

The still-modest size and endurance of the First World War destroyer tended to limit it very much to duties closely connected with major bodies of the fleet. Where enemy territory was reasonably close, however, independent light forces were set up, such as Tyrwhitt's Harwich Force and the famous Dover Patrol, both of which were continuously engaged against enemy destroyer forays in the Channel and southern North Sea. In their smaller craft, the Germans set a high standard of gunnery, and a couple of the U.K.–Norway convoys were very severely handled by enemy destroyers.

The mass torpedo attacks, so much practised and written about in prewar days, failed largely to materialise as the large fleet action, with the exception of Jutland, did not occur. Nevertheless, on that occasion, the threat posed by a

opposite
The Darings were the end of a line of
British destroyer development spanning
three quarters of a century, giving way
to the more versatile frigate. H.M.S.
Diamond is seen here in 1957.

right
The wide-spread funnels of the 1905
French destroyer *Oriflamme* betray boiler
rooms separated by machinery spaces.
The smoke nuisance caused to fleet
gunnery officers by a large number of
escort destroyers can also be guessed-at!

below
These Japanese Kaba-class destroyers, in
company with an early French armoured
cruiser, show how international the basic
destroyer design had become by the
First World War.

feint from Scheer's destroyers was
sufficient to force Jellicoe's battleships to turn away; it was this
move, more than any other, which
cost the Grand Fleet the decision
that it sought on that frustrating
day.

As the U.S. Navy did not get
involved in European waters until
1917, the designers of their
destroyers had little practical war
experience. This could account for
the enormous number of flush-
decked, 'four-pipers', that they
went on to produce. Best described
as fast and fragile, they lacked the
robust weatherliness of the contemporary British V & W classes
then entering service. These latter
distinctive ships, with their thick
and thin funnels of unequal height,
adopted superimposed guns fore
and aft (together with a 3-inch A/A
gun) and established the basic
destroyer layout which endured
world-wide until the end of the

destroyer itself. The Modified W's
exchanged the 4-inch gun for the
4.7-inch together with tripled torpedo tubes, and their leaders provided the basis for successive
flotillas from 'A' to 'I' which were
built up to 1938 with little modifi-
cation. The design was simple but
sound.

The American 'four-pipers' were
so prolific that they formed the U.S.
fleet's destroyer force through to
the early 1930s, when the Farraguts
introduced a European-type raised
forecastle layout, together with the
5-inch 38 that was retained as their
standard destroyer gun until 1943.
They did, however, mount 12
torpedo tubes against only eight
in contemporary British ships.

This rather orthodox series of
ships contrasted sharply with
French practice which favoured
the 'super-destroyer'. As early as
1924 the Tigre class topped 2,100
tons and carried five 5.1-inch guns

at over 35 knots. Within 10 years,
they had progressed to the Fan-
tasque and Mogador classes, which
carried eight 5.5-inch weapons on a
3,000-ton hull at speeds up to 40
knots.

These were in reply to the large
Italian Navigatori's, though in
general the Italians kept closely to
the small torpedo boat idea. With
the Japanese also having produced
the Hibikis and the Germans the
Maass and her sisters, which had
five 5-inch guns on a 2,250-ton
standard displacement, the British
were moved to reply. With experience in the design and construction
of larger destroyers for export
(notably to Poland and Yugoslavia)
the jump to the 1,870-ton Tribal
class of 1938 was not difficult.
These 16 ships doubled the gun
armament to eight 4.7-inch at the
expense of one set of torpedo
tubes. Although these were
'specials', the standard flotilla ships

too were up-graded after the I-class, with the 'J' and 'K' types having six guns in three twin mountings, together with a full set of ten torpedo tubes. The following 'L' and 'M'-classes should all have received large new power-operated gunhouses but early shortages resulted in a half-flotilla of 'L's being equipped with eight 4-inch HA guns in twin mountings.

The Second World War, from the point of view of the destroyer, was very different from the First. In the earlier conflict their modest size and endurance had limited them to fleet support and near-seas work, but the ships of 1939 were capable of far more independent action. The more modern, high performance units were allocated to fleet work, leaving the more elderly ships for tasks such as convoy escort. Where, in 1914–18, the war at sea had been almost lost before the convoy system was adopted, the protection of merchant shipping was organised from the outset in 1939. Escorts were immediately at a premium and more and more destroyers were pressed into service for duties for which they were ill-suited.

What was required was a simple, medium-speed ship of high capacity and endurance and the destroyer was none of these. The prime enemy was the submarine, so guns and torpedo tubes were reduced in favour of extra depth charges and radar. In some of the veteran V and W's – now in their second war – the forward boiler room was gutted in favour of extra bunker space and accommodation. They looked a little strange, having shed their forward funnel, but these doughty little ships could still make 25 knots, having the range and 'legs' of the new frigates, purpose-built for the job.

Making its appearance also was the Hunt-class escort destroyer, designed to combine both A/A and A/S functions in a small hull. This it did successfully, although

below
Rotterdam-built ships, naval and mercantile, traditionally berth on the Parkkade prior to trials. HNMS *Holland* was nameship of one of the last classes of conventional destroyers built in the West.

early ships were extremely tender. The U.S. Navy also instituted an incredible programme of destroyer escorts, or DEs. Over 1,000 were ordered, of which 565 were completed. These were to several designs, mainly because of the wide range of machinery that was installed. Even the industrial capacity of the United States was taxed by orders of this magnitude and, besides diesel and steam turbine ships there were groups using diesel- and turbo-electric propulsion, very expensive installations which, however, by-passed the need for gearboxes, the want of which had put turbo-electric machinery into many American battleships. The only common propulsion system not used seemed to be the humble reciprocating steam engine, favoured by the British for its simplicity and reliability and included in many of the lower performance frigates. Both the Hunts and the DEs fell into a zone which was neither true destroyer nor frigate and the DE was built by the U.S. almost to the exclusion of frigates.

In the war, the mass destroyer torpedo attack was a manoeuvre more of theory than of practice although classic attacks were carried out by smaller groups, notably on the *Bismarck* and the *Haguro*. In the bitter night battles around the Solomons, the Japanese destroyers proved formidable opponents, their prodigal use of torpedoes being a constant menace.

The British, like the Japanese, established a great moral superiority over their enemies by virtue of their great aggression, even to the point of self-sacrifice. For instance, the *Acasta*'s torpedoing of *Scharnhorst*, *Glowworm* ramming *Hipper*, and Warburton-Lee's action at Narvik all followed within the space of a few weeks. The most deadly opponents of the destroyer proved to be aircraft and the submarine, neither of which she was designed to counter.

Although it was becoming apparent that the less-glamorous frigate would eventually be the more useful, the destroyer was by no means dead and vast numbers were built under the war emergency programmes. The Ameri-

left
Early destroyer men earned a bonus known as 'hard-lying money', the justice of which is here graphically demonstrated in the Bay of Biscay. The destroyer is H.M.S. *Tetrarch*, an improved 'Admiralty R' and typical of the Grand Fleet escorts of the First World War.

below
At 2,900 tons, the Japanese destroyer *Yubari* was something of a phenomenon in 1923. The large, twinned gun mountings and typically Japanese funnel and forward sheerline are clear in this 1937 picture, taken at Shanghai.

below
The large force of war-built American destroyers was given an extension of life by modernisation under the FRAM programmes. Many have since been transferred to friendly navies and the ex-Sumner-class *Hugh Purvis* is here seen as the Turkish *Zafer*.

bottom
The Royal Navy's Type 42 is an excellent all-round destroyer. All gas turbine propelled, her armament includes the Seadart SAM and a Lynx helicopter. Here is H.M.S. *Sheffield*.

cans, particularly, turned out long production runs. The near-100 Bensons, of 1,700 tons, mounted four 5-inch guns and were direct descendants of the earlier Farraguts. From 1940, they were followed by more than 170 Fletchers. These reverted to the flush deck and the addition of a fifth gun took their tonnage above 2,000. About 60 Sumners came next, packing six 5-inch guns by adopting twin gun-houses, and these were finally refined into the 2,400-ton Gearing class, similar in layout but 'stretched' to give greater endurance and seaworthiness.

The Royal Navy's war zones demanded a smaller type of destroyer and about 100 were built, standardised at about 1,700-tons and armed with four, single 4.7-inch guns (later 4.5-inch) and eight or ten torpedo tubes. With minor variations, the succeeding flotillas from 'O' to 'Z' and followed by four groups of C's, represented a simple and reliable type of ship. They were good seaboats and could always use their guns, compared with the Sumners, which were over-gunned and exhibited structural weaknesses and excessive motion under the weight of armament.

By 1942, plans were being formulated to re-form a British Pacific Fleet, which called for a larger type of destroyer. Of the planned 40 Battle class, only 24 were completed, mostly after the end of the war. They were interesting in having their main battery forward in a new type of twin 4.5-inch gun-house and a heavy, radar-laid A/A armament of 40 mm guns aft to counter constant threat of air attack in the Far East.

Parallel with the Battles came the Weapons. These were designed to provide a fast A/S screen and mounted only 4-inch calibre armament to complement two ahead-throwing triple-barrelled Squid mortars. These could put a pattern of bombs accurately on to a submerged target whilst it was in the ASDIC beam. The earlier depth charge had, of course, to be dropped blind as a ship passed over its quarry's estimated position.

Later war-built German destroyers shipped an armament of five 5.9-inch guns on a 2,600-ton hull. Credited with 38 knots speed, they could have proved a major nuisance had they been imaginatively used.

The substantial Russian destroyer force was reinforced by ships transferred from the Allies, but achieved little. Some of their impotence could possibly be ascribed to the debilitating effect of Stalin's pre-war purges (cf. the French post-revolutionary navy); the rest probably had political causes.

By the end of the war, the conventional destroyer had reached the end of its road. The British slowly completed the big Darings, but neither they nor the Americans laid down any more. However several European navies built notable classes such as the French Surcoufs and successive Swedish classes which culminated in the magnificent Östergötlands. A surprise of the 1950s was the large group of Skoryis produced by the Russians. Over 70 were built and gave warning of the expansion to come but, like their cruisers, they were obsolescent on completion as the Americans already had a Terrier SAM system in the converted Gearing-class destroyer *Gyatt*, and had the Adams and Coontz classes laid down. The British had ordered the large County class with a Seaslug SAM and, significantly, a helicopter in place of the A/S mortars originally planned.

These SAM destroyers were designed to counter the high-flying aircraft carrying a stand-off nuclear bomb, which posed the major threat to the carrier groups then forming the western fleets' main striking force. The most likely aggressors in those uneasy years of the Cold War were the Russians, but the fleet that they were expanding lacked a base of carrier-borne airpower, of which they had no experience. They expanded around the submarine and such warships as were necessary to keep enemy carriers outside airstrike range.

To give their ships greater potential they developed the surface-to-surface missile, or SSM, and it was these, rather than SAMs which they first had at sea. Known to the West as Scrubber and later, Shaddock, these missiles were capable of ranges of up to 200 miles. As this was well over the horizon of ship-borne radar, the Russians had to develop new methods of active terminal guidance within the missile and mid-course correction by use of ship-borne helicopter. In acting offensively against a carrier group, however, they needed also SAMs for self-defence against the inevitable air strike that would follow and the 17-mile ranged Goa made its appearance.

Well aware of the potential threat that the new Russian submarine fleet posed to its mercantile fleets, the West developed new A/S weaponry. The homing torpedo was the most effective but had limited power for pursuing its high-speed prey. It needed to be dropped close to its target and the means of doing this was either by ship-borne helicopter or by ASROC. This eight-celled launcher was designed to fire a vehicle out to about 6 miles range, carrying either a homing torpedo or a nuclear depth charge to the target area before releasing it. Similar weapons are the Australian Ikara and the French Malafon.

To fill the gap until new classes were available, both the Americans and the British converted many war-built destroyers to an A/S role. In the FRAM programme, many of the U.S. destroyers exchanged the greater part of their original armament in favour of ASROC, A/S torpedoes and DASH (Drone Anti-Submarine Helicopter) systems. The last of these proved unreliable and was abandoned, robbing the ships of much of their effectiveness as they had not the potential for operating larger, manned helicopters.

The British conversions were re-designated 'frigates', the Type 15 being the full conversion and the Type 16 partial. About this time the distinction between destroyer and frigate was sometimes

only a matter of nomenclature. Destroyers, if anything, tended to be larger and faster if used for duties with a task group rather than everyday escort work, and grew to a size rather larger than some earlier cruisers. This latter term changed to cover generally those ships of larger tonnage with duplicate missile systems, able to engage several targets simultaneously. None of these terms is precise, however, and they tend to overlap.

Under the guidance of Gorsh-

top
The complexity and size of the Russian Kashin class takes them beyond the true destroyer concept. The armament fit is designed for the engagement of surface, submarine and aerial targets.

above
One of the most successful Russian multi-role destroyers is the Krivak type. Besides the large launchers forward, which fire anti-ship or anti-submarine missiles, a further twin SAM launcher is retracted into the inconspicuous silo forward of the turrets.

kov, the Russian fleet has expanded rapidly with a preponderance of small classes of ship. The exceptions are the Kashin and Krivak classes. The former introduced the gas turbine at an early date, with its advantages of immediate power on demand, compactness, repair by replacement and ease of automation. The Krivaks demonstrate the Russian trend towards multifunction ships, being armed with a large quadruple SSM launcher, two fast-reaction SAM launchers, two 12-barrelled A/S rocket projectors, two quadruple banks of torpedo tubes and four 76 mm DP guns. As all this is carried on a displacement of only about 4,000 tons it is not surprising that no helicopter is carried, although this is usual with Soviet destroyers, only larger units having room for anything more than a basic flight pad.

Having such tremendous strike capacity in their carriers, the Americans were late in developing SSMs and in putting helicopters into their destroyers. The rapid reduction in numbers of available carriers has, however, forced these trends

upon them. Starting with the 1964 Belknaps (since re-rated as cruisers) they began a reduction in missile armament to allow space for full helicopter facilities. This, in turn, has stimulated development of multi-purpose launchers which can fire both A/A and A/S missiles (and maybe later SSM in addition). The possible drawback to the necessarily extremely complex magazine feed arrangements is the risk that a single fault may rob a ship of its major armament systems.

The western European navies, because of their lack of carriers, developed expertise in helicopter and SSM much earlier. In the French-built *Exocet* they have a 20-mile anti-ship missile that hugs the surface during its final flight phase to prevent detection by and counter-measures from its target. Dependent upon its guidance system a missile can be jammed by ECM (Electronic Counter Measures) or foxed by decoys. It can also be shot down by anti-missile missiles, such as the fast-reaction British Seawolf or by

Close-in Weapon Systems, which are rotating, multi-barrel Gatling-type guns which rely on saturation by fragments of the airspace through which the missile has to fly. Both America and Russia use these systems.

The Japanese navy (known as the Maritime Self-Defence Force) is particularly A/S-orientated, but has developed destroyer-type ships for the purpose, rather than frigates. As if to underline its future the U.S. Navy is commissioning the extended Spruance class. Almost identical in size with the 6,600-ton *Belknaps*, they have retained their 'destroyer' title, probably because they lack a medium-range missile system. Their massive hulls appear under-armed but have great space potential for interchange of weapon systems.

H.M.S. *Devonshire* fires one of her Seaslug SAMs. This rather cumbersome weapon was the Royal Navy's first major missile, but has now been superseded by the more compact Seadart.

The Frigate

Escort vessels, as opposed to destroyers, did not emerge as a type until the development of the submarine threat against merchant shipping during the First World War. They were produced in large numbers but were ineffective because, as long as their quarry remained submerged, they had to rely on rather primitive hydrophones for detection and lacked a suitable anti-submarine weapon until the rather tardy introduction of the depth charge, at that time a slow-sinking device with a rather erratic hydrostatic detonator. Single charges could fairly easily be dodged by an agile submarine and the 'pattern' of up to 14 charges was the standard even up to 1944 in order to give a reasonable chance of a 'kill'. It was not until the 1920s that the 'Asdic' was developed by the Royal Navy, the few sets being so precious that they were, for long, the province of fleet destroyers only. This device emitted regular bursts of energy along a fairly narrow beam ahead of the ships. Any 'target' in its path would produce an echo, the effect of which could be detected by the ship and amplified to an audible 'ping'. The effect was followed down the track, and the time for returning echoes gave a means of measuring the range. As the beam was focussed ahead, contact was always lost as the ship ran over the target to drop its depth charges.

The requirements of electronics for navigation, surveillance, target acquisition and communications result in a mass of antenna competing for limited mast space.

right

The Kil-class escorts of 1917–18 were designed with a double-ended profile so that a submarine would have difficulty in establishing their true course. They were of about 900 tons displacement and all forty had names beginning with 'Kil'.

below

The Flower-class escorts of the First World War were as prolific as those in the Second. Most acted as sloops, with some minesweeping capacity, but many were converted into the so-called Q-ships in the hope that their rather mercantile appearance would delude unwary submarines into a surface attack.

An alert submarine commander could detect this and make an abrupt change in course.

Asdic transducers trainable in azimuth were later introduced, but the break of contact remained a problem, unsolved until the introduction of the ahead-throwing mortars, such as Mousetrap and Hedgehog, in the Second World War.

The first extended class of escort ship was the 1915 Flower class, over 70 1,200-tonners built to mercantile class for speed of construction and many, indeed, looking like merchant ships. They were later classified as Sloops but were built as Fleet Sweeping Vessels, a dual function that bedevilled escort ship design to beyond 1940. The following '24' class, named after racehorses (H.M.S. *Spearmint* and H.M.S. *Isinglass* being particularly hard to accept!) were more A/S-orientated and built with a profile deliberately designed to make their true course difficult to establish. They had a dazzle-painted hull with straight stem and stern, a single funnel amidships and identical superstructure masses on either side. The single mast was placed forward of the funnel in some ships, abaft it in others. This idea was extended in the later 'Kil' class.

More like warships were the minesweeping sloops of the Hunt class. When the mine became a major menace, many trawlers and

drifters were commissioned into the fleet to supplement the regular ships. They performed an invaluable service but one of their drawbacks was a dangerously large draught for moving in mined waters. To counter this the Atherstone class paddlers and the Dance class were built, the latter having their propellers in tunnels, giving a draught of less than four feet. The guns shipped by these smaller units were various, but those with 4-inch or 4.7-inch guns often doubled as escorts and provided the basic pattern for the sloops and *aviso*'s built largely for colonial duties between the wars by Britain and France.

By about 1936, danger of war was growing and, with memories of convoys of the 1914–18 war still quite fresh, plans were made for the next generation of escorts. Aircraft had, by now, developed as a serious threat as well as the submarine. To counter this, the A/A sloop with six HA 4-inch guns was evolved through to the Black Swan groups. These were excellent little all-rounders with good A/S potential. Some of the class were also expected to have minelaying capacity and some even that of minesweeping!

A/S thinking went in two directions. The first produced the Hunt-class escort destroyers already dealt with and, the other, another mercantile-based escort, known as a Corvette. These were another

Flower class, simple reciprocating-engined ships with a hull based on that of a whale-catcher. Incredibly lively at sea, hundreds were built both in the U.K. and Canada and bore the brunt of the early North Atlantic convoy war, a conflict in which the Royal Canadian Navy came of age.

One drawback of the corvette was its lack of speed, which meant it could only really remain on station in a convoy's screen leaving destroyers to do the chasing. Another disadvantage was its lack

top
Nearly 50 of the rakish P-boats were built for close-range patrol duties in the First World War. They were armed with a 4-inch gun and depth charges and their turbines were good for about 23 knots. They were surprisingly good seaboats and their shallow draught made them particularly useful in mined areas.

above
The vast fleet of escorts created during the Second World War was largely superfluous to requirements after the close of hostilities. Harwich was one of many ports with sad 'trots' of once-proud warships. Castle, River and Algerine classes await disposal.

of capacity; with U-boat attacks coordinated over several days, prodigious quantities of depth charges could be expended. Its limited range required refuelling at sea or an early return to port if this was not possible, and its liveliness was extremely exhausting for its crew.

Obviously, a large escort was needed urgently. Where American thought produced the destroyer-escort (already dealt with) the British introduced the River class, which bore the newly resurrected title of Frigate, a historically incorrect classification that has remained ever since. Nearly 100 feet longer than the Flowers, they were built in large numbers not only in the U.K. but also in Canada and the U.S.A. Of twice the power and better armed, they took much of the sheer misery from the escort man's lot.

Although small A/S craft were produced by both Italy and Japan during the war, neither succeeded in building in the required quantity or with technological excellence enough to stem the submarine onslaughts mounted against their merchant shipping. Successive refinements of A/S escorts were largely a British province with the Americans concentrating on DEs. Although the Flowers were enlarged into the Castles, these handsome little ships proved to be the last of the wartime corvettes, overtaken by the frigate with its superior capabilities. The Rivers were superseded by the Loch and Bay classes, whose respective A/S and A/A armaments were interchangeable on a common hull. The

above
Warships have an important rôle in peacetime in both ceremonial and 'showing the flag'. Here the Leander class frigate *Phoebe* makes a brave sight at the 1969 Torbay Review.

right
Earlier classes of post-Second War RN frigates featured superstructures of deliberately low profile. The example shown is H.M.S. *Londonderry* of the Type 12 A/S class.

escorts, together with aircraft, were absolutely crucial in keeping the convoy routes open; without them the Allies could never have prosecuted the war.

The failure by the German Navy to produce advanced A/S ships was not of great importance to them as they were engaged in a largely land-based war. It could be argued, however, that an efficient Italian A/S force could have fought convoys across to North Africa in 1942 and the defeats of El Alamein and after may never have been suffered – for the Royal Navy defeated Rommel as surely as it had defeated Napoleon, neither of whom ever saw the cause of his discomfiture but felt its presence in the lack of essential supplies.

Japan, a mercantile power, should have put a higher priority on the production of A/S ships.

However, she had not been taught the bitter lessons of 1917 as had Britain, and when she built, she built too late. The American submarine fleet practised a blockade every bit as deadly as that of the British and, with the loss of their merchantmen, the Japanese lost their island war.

The U.S. Navy ended the war with such a number of DEs that they formed the basis of its A/S

above
Reloading a depth-charge thrower on a Second World War escort. Understandably, the rate of delivery on to a submerged target was low, aggravated by the weapon's low rate of sinkage due to a total lack of hydrodynamic shape.

right
U.S. escort production during the Second World War was geared to the destroyer escort (DE) rather than the true frigate. 565 were completed, many being transferred to allied navies including nearly 80 to the RN. All these were named after famous captains and shown here is H.M.S. *Bentinck* of the turbo-electric Buckley class.

above
The clean lines of the Type 21 frigate *Ambuscade* are shown to advantage as she goes down the ways at the Yarrow yard, formerly known for its fine destroyers.

left
The rakish lines of the Type 21 frigate *Amazon* mark her out as a commercial design. She was a product of the yard of Vosper Thornycroft and is typical of a range of successful designs produced by them.

right, above
The French A/S frigate *Le Lorrain* carries no less than twelve torpedo tubes in addition to the mortar forward. These are augmented by a useful 57mm gun armament.

right, lower
The British A/S frigate *Lowestoft* pitches in a cross sea. The excellent sea-keeping qualities of such ships are a tribute to careful research work and tank-testing in shore establishments.

force for the better part of another decade, being improved only with the short Dealey class. The other Allied navies that had been actively involved in the Battle of the Atlantic seemed to take the new build-up of the Russian submarine fleet rather more seriously, developing further escort classes that incorporated battle experience. The Royal Navy rebuilt many Second World War destroyers into Type 15 frigates whose main features, long forecastles, small surface armament and two A/S mortars, were also those of the Type 12's.

The Canadians at this time were building the individual St. Laurents and the French the Le Corse class, the latter being much closer to the frigate concept. Interesting British sub classes were the Types 41 and 61, for A/A defence and aircraft direction respectively. Their specialist functions were soon overtaken by the introduction of the SAM and more compact electronics, small enough to be fitted to any ship required to control aircraft. Again, making up in technique what they lacked in numbers, the British had manned helicopters operating from the Type 81 (Tribal) class GP frigates of the early 'sixties. Each of the class also had gas turbine cruising machinery.

The Black Swans were originally rated as A/A sloops. They were built to an extremely high standard and proved that their dual-purpose gun armament was complemented by an excellent A/S capacity. H.M.S. *Cygnet* is seen here in Baltic waters.

The River class were the first of a new breed of escort, designed for North Atlantic conditions. The name 'frigate' was re-introduced with them in 1941 and shown here is H.M.S. *Test*.

The Russian navy first concentrated on destroyers when they resumed construction postwar. Not until 1952 did they commence the 40 or so Riga-class ships. Of about 1,200 tons standard and 28 knots, with a good surface armament, including torpedo tubes and mine-laying ability, they were more truly escort destroyers than frigates, corresponding to the British Hunts of the Second World War. It should be remembered, of course, that convoy escorts, of the type needed by the NATO-alliance navies, are not required by Russia.

She is self-sufficient and her merchant marine, although a weapon of considerable political economic power, is not essential to her survival. In any conflict, it would virtually disappear from the seas except for operations in conjunction with the regular fleet.

After the Riga class, the Russians built the smaller Petya and Mirka classes, interesting little 1,000-tonners with diesel propulsion that can rapidly be boosted by gas turbines when speed is required for an attack. These have been further refined into the still smaller Grisha class ships, some of which are equipped with the fast-response SA-N-4 SAM system, enabling them to operate inshore under hostile airspace.

The failure of the American DASH drone helicopter system made the U.S. Navy increase its reliance on its ASROC in the absence of air support. Although an excellent weapon, it depended upon hull-mounted sonars (which are affected by noise at all but low ship speeds) or variable depth sonars (VDS) whose use is limited in shallow waters. Obviously, there was no really good alternative to the manned helicopter, which was incorporated in the Knox class of 1969. Although criticised for its single-screw propulsion, the design has been successively improved from the prototype pair of Bronsteins of 1963 to the current (1977) Perry class. Their major features deserve comparison:

1. Bronstein (1963): Length, 372 feet: Guns: DASH helicopter: ASROC
2. Garcia (1964–8): Length, 415 feet: Guns: DASH helicopter: ASROC
3. Knox (1969–74): Length, 438 feet: Guns: Manned helicopter: ASROC: short range SAM
4. Perry (1977 on): Length, 445 feet: Guns: CIWS: Two manned helicopters: Medium range SAM/SSM.

It will be noted how, in the latest class, the presence of two helicopters has encouraged the designers to dispense with the ASROC system. Each helicopter is large enough to carry radar, sonobuoys and dunking sonar for pinpointing a submerged target and torpedoes for destroying it. Electronics are being developed to enable a group of ships and their helicopters to work as a coordinated team by the constant interchange of data; this combination should go far to offset the advantages of the high-speed submarine.

The ever-shrinking resources of the Royal Navy have become increasingly devoted to A/S warfare as its world-wide interests have gradually been exchanged for those of NATO. The extensive Leander class was based on the Type 12. Superb seaboats, they were becoming outmoded until rearmed with Exocet SSMs or Ikara, although they are still lacking a modern A/A system. Their successors, the Type 21 Amazons, are the first commercially designed frigates to serve in the Royal Navy since the Second

This aerial view of the A/S frigate *Leander* shows clearly the Ikara in its zareba forward, the helicopter deck aft, with the Limbo mortar and variable depth sonar (VDS) in their respective wells.

World War. They are COGOG ships which have proved very satisfactory all-rounders. Although they ship only one helicopter, it is the Anglo-French Lynx, a great improvement on the little Wasp of earlier classes. The new Type 22, or Battleaxe, class will ship two helicopters like the excellent Canadian Tribals and Italian Andace's, but will be classed as destroyers, in spite of their specialist design. One unfortunate aspect of the Type 22's is the total lack of any major calibre gun, and that at a time when a gun's greater flexibility over that of missiles is becoming recognised and the U.S. Navy is experimenting with a lightweight 8-inch weapon to confer greater firepower upon its smaller warships.

The general trend is for the 'first division' navies to concentrate on larger, multi-system frigates that can operate worldwide. The lesser fleets have capitalised on the increasing lethality of modern missile systems by incorporating them in smaller 'corvette' type ships which, for a comparatively small financial outlay, could well deny major navies access to important inshore routes such as the Baltic entrances, Red Sea, Bosphorus, etc.

top
The Type 14 A/S frigate *Exmouth*, as rebuilt as a testbed for the Olympus gas turbine. Experience gained formed the basis for subsequent Royal Navy all-gas-turbine warships.

above
Both helicopters and gas turbines were introduced into British frigate design with the Tribal class. Shown here is the first-of-class, *Ashanti,* commissioned in in 1961.

Miscellaneous Classes

No treatment of the history of the warship would be complete without mentioning the smaller or more specialist classes that have been evolved against particular requirements. One such was the Monitor. Starting with the American ship of that name, the term was originally applied to a low-freeboard turret ship, usually heavily protected. As such, it became synonymous with coast defence ships, notable examples of which were built in Britain for the Australian States. Development was then toward a more seaworthy type which could be termed 'pocket cruisers' and built particularly for the Baltic navies and Thailand. These carried a small number of useful-calibre guns, up to 10-inch, on a shallow draught hull.

The Royal Navy, fighting in every conceivable theatre, built them in considerable numbers for inshore use during the First World War. Three 1,260-tonners building in the U.K. for Brazil were taken over at the outbreak of war and given River names. Small ships and armed only with 6-inch and 4.7-inch guns, they had been designed for river work, and soon proved their worth by penetrating the Rufiji delta to despatch the German raider *Königsberg* which had gone to earth there.

The two Gorgons, that followed with 9.2-inch guns, were building for Norway and more truly coast-defence ships. The quartette of Abercrombies, at over 6,000 tons, were completed in 1915 and the largest to date. They each had a pair of 14-inch guns, procured at short notice from the U.S.A., where they had been manufactured for a

Greek battle cruiser which was to have been built in Germany! All monitors tended to be 'scratch' vessels and armed with whatever guns were available. Thus the 19 'M' class ships for inshore work mounted a mixture of 9.2-inch, 7.5-inch, 6-inch or 4.7-inch guns, all old and brought out of store. The 6,000-ton Lord Clives were given old 12-inch guns from pre-Dreadnoughts, whose effectiveness

top
Thornycroft built Torpedo Boat No. 2 in 1878. She was of only 33 tons displacement but mounted not only a trainable torpedo tube forward but also dropping gear amidships.

above
The British monitor *Mersey*, and her sister-ship *Severn*, destroyed the blockaded German cruiser *Königsberg* in the Rufiji in 1915. Note the low-freeboard hull and high control position. Highflyer-class protected cruiser in background.

141

opposite, top
Rapid loading of depth charge throwers on the heaving deck of a second World War armed trawler called for great care and careful teamwork.

opposite, lower
Apparently defunct types of warship sometimes return in a new guise. These miniature armoured monitors were part of a considerable rivurine fleet operated by the Americans in Vietnam.

below
The Dutch colonial gunboat *Flores* dated from 1925, and her three 5.9-inch guns were still valuable at the Normandy landings in 1944.

bottom
H.M.S. *Lurcher* was one of three 'Special I'-class launched by Yarrow in 1912. She easily achieved 34 knots and, fitted with long range W/T equipment, served at Harwich during the First World War.

was so low that it was necessary to make a decision that some of the 15-inch weapons urgently needed for the new battleships would have to be appropriated.

Apart from their guns, monitors were supremely simple ships. They were very beamy, incorporating large bulges, which gave them some degree of torpedo protection as well as ballast capacity, and by flooding them on one side they could be listed to give extra elevation for their guns. They were incredibly slow, often good for only 6 knots when clean, and sometimes being forced to anchor in a strong tidal stream. With such a low performance they were usable only in uncontested sea areas and their duties were primarily gunfire

support for the army's flank; their mainly army-type names reflect this connection. Common recognition features were the spotting top on a lofty tripod mast, and the large amount of turret barbette exposed because of the shallow hull construction.

The Marshal Ney's were the first 15-inch ships, with a more rational secondary armament of eight 4-inch guns. They were, surprisingly for 1915, diesel-propelled, but could still not reach 7 knots! The last of those completed during the First World War were the two Terrors, with the same armament as the Marshals but enlarged to accommodate triple expansion machinery for 14 knots. Late in the war, three of the Lord Clives were given an 18-inch gun apiece from the ill-starred Furious programme. These were mounted aft, in addition to the 12-inch guns forward. The big gun was housed on a non-rotating mounting, being trained permanently to starboard and capable of varying only its elevation.

Most monitors were scrapped soon after the war but the *Marshal Soult* and the two Terrors survived for service in the Second World War. The army situation was much more fluid than in 1914–18 and most active sea areas were now liable to attack from enemy aircraft, so that there was far less use for the monitor. In spite of this, the two 8,000-ton Abercrombies of 1942 were constructed, of which the *Roberts* had the dubious distinction of being the last British warship to carry the fine 15-inch gun. With her scrapping in 1968 the monitor – a peculiarly British warship – came to the end of its road.

In direct contrast to the lumbering progress of the monitor was the speed of nearly 40 knots attained by some Coastal Motor Boats, or CMBs. These were developed primarily by Thornycroft from pre-war hull-forms and designed to drop 18-inch torpedoes over the stern. They were of 45, 55 or 70 feet in length, the larger types being capable of carrying depth charges or mines as an alternative to torpedoes. Their early frailty

inhibited their potential; they were built of wood and proved particularly prone to fire from their petrol engines and vulnerable to attack from the air.

The Royal Navy's largely-forgotten war in the Baltic after the armistice of 1918 enabled the CMB to show its possibilities in the attack on the fortified Russian base at Kronstadt.

Interest lapsed between the wars but was revived in the mid-1930s. By the outbreak of war the British had the Vosper 70-foot hard-chine boat in service. These were now known as Motor Torpedo Boats, or MTBs, and of wooden construction. They carried two torpedoes but were still propelled by petrol engines. The Italian Navy developed the fast MAS boats with a round-bilge hull form, bearing in mind the possibility of A/S work. Even the U.S. Navy was building the so-called PT boat, developed from a British prototype, but the most seaworthy examples proved to be the German S-boats, commonly known as E-boats. They were larger than their British equivalents, of round-bilge form and having a higher forecastle deck, under which the torpedo tubes were situated, firing forward through bow doors. Their weatherliness and endurance enabled them to operate extensively off England's east coast, constantly disrupting the coastal convoys. They could also lay mines and had the great advantage of being diesel propelled, greatly reducing the fire risk.

British MTB squadrons were used offensively, too, against their German opposite numbers, with neither side ever gaining permanent ascendancy. Axis coastal trade was also attacked, together with any larger targets that presented themselves. Notable successes were the German sinking of the British cruiser *Charybdis* and her escort and the British torpedoing of the German raider *Komet*.

The British firm of Fairmile also produced a useful range of boats, including the ubiquitous MLs (C-type) and the larger Motor Gun Boats, or MGBs (D-type), which could be armed either with torpedoes or with guns, some of them mounting a short-barrelled 4.5-inch howitzer.

British coastal forces were used extensively as far afield as Norway and the Adriatic and in specialised operations, such as the St. Nazaire

top, left
West German M40-class minesweepers on an exercise. They were war-built but retained by the Germans post-war to start the clearance of their mine-infested coasts. Nearest the camera are *Seehund* and *Seeigel*.

top, right
One of the ubiquitous Landing Craft, Tank or LCT, shown during the Normandy operations of 1944. Visible are the bow ramp and heavy kedge anchor aft.

above
An American PT boat shown in the Solomons during the Japanese war. Island-studded waters such as these are ideal for the use of fast attack craft.

opposite, top
Seapower includes the projection and support of power ashore. The Allied command of English Channel waters cannot be better epitomised than by this aerial view of the Mulberry harbour established on the Normandy coast in 1944.

raid. It was not all one-sided however, with the Italians using their MAS boats to harass the Malta convoys and even attacking Valletta itself. They also torpedoed the heavy cruiser *York* at Crete.

American PT boats were particularly active in the Philippines where the island-studded seas suited their hit-and-run type of warfare. One oddity was the British Steam Gun Boat, or SGB, which proved quiet but extremely vulnerable to any form of action damage.

After the Second World War the 'mosquito navies' were rapidly sold out of service and interest again languished. This situation was suddenly reversed in the late 1950s by Russia's development of the SS-N-2 (Styx) missile, capable of being carried by Fast Patrol Boats, as the type was now called. Their Komar and Osa classes house these missiles in two or four bins respectively. Their range is over 20 miles and, as the projectiles home automatically with active radar or infra-red heads, no bulky guidance radar needed to be carried by the launching craft itself.

Being relatively inexpensive, boats of this type have proved popular with the smaller navies, providing building nations such as Britain, Germany and France with good export markets and the opportunity to acquire expertise. The tendency has been to increase their size to the point where the term 'Guided Missile Corvette' is being adopted. They are now usually of metal construction and either diesel or gas turbine pro-

pelled. Typical of these new craft are the Russian Nanutchkas of about 800 tons, armed with six SSMs, short range SAMs and guns. In a smaller bracket are such classes as the Swedish Jageren, the German Typ 143 and the French Combattant. However, although these craft are built by countries with major fleets they are not often operated by them as they rarely fit in with the requirements of the peacetime 'blue water' navies.

Other directions of development include both the hydrofoils and hovercraft, both of which increase speeds dramatically by lifting the hull clear of the water, reducing skin friction. It is in this general area that the greatest advances in warship technology are likely in the near future. Small, agile craft such as these, armed with high-powered missiles, may well prove very difficult for the conventional surface ship to counter. Their best protection would currently appear to lie in the helicopter armed with a purpose-designed air-to-surface missile, such as the Sea Skua and a Seaspray-type radar to give high definition in adverse conditions.

Amphibious warfare has spawned all manner of craft. Throughout history one of a navy's prime functions has been the landing of armies wherever may be required, and then assuring the necessary control of the sea to sustain that military presence as long as may be necessary. For the most part, the fleet used its own boats for the task, but this was possible only as long as the army

remained primarily an infantry force. Twentieth-century wars added much heavy impedimenta and specialised craft became necessary. Some of the first of these were the motor-driven 'Beetles' used at the Dardanelles in 1915, but it took the Second World War to stimulate rapid development. The problem was how to put fully equipped men, their artillery, armour and vehicles ashore 'over the beach', without the preliminaries of capturing a major port, or in places where no ports existed, such as the Pacific islands. A simple, flat-bottomed, boxy craft with a bow ramp provided the basis of most designs. The little assault landing craft, or LCA, set a pattern, with 'cargo' space forward and all machinery aft. The next was the Landing Craft, Tank or LCT, a diesel-driven 150-footer, tailor-made to transport three medium tanks. These were large enough to have superstructure aft, above the machinery space. To keep their bows square on to the beach and to avoid broaching in the surf, a kedge anchor was laid out over the stern during the approach. This was later used to pull the craft off the beach by means of the winch.

For more distant operations the Landing Ship, Tank was evolved from the LCT. It was very similar in concept but over twice as long, and as an alternative to vehicles it could carry smaller fully-laden landing craft. It loaded these simply by opening the clam-shell style bow doors, ballasting down and floating them in. The reverse process

left
The British Amphibious Warfare Ship *Bulwark* was formerly a conventional carrier. She now operates only helicopters and STOL aircraft in an assault capacity, although a certain amount of A/S capability exists.

below
Fleet auxiliaries of the Royal Navy. The lead ship is *Resource*, built to replenish armament and dry stores of HM ships. The large fleet tanker following has RAS hoses rigged at the gantries.

opposite, top
Light forces contesting the narrow seas during the Second World War were operated not only by the Royal Navy but also by Allied forces in exile, as the Dutch flag here testifies. Note the 20mm Oerlikon, 0.5-inch MGs and flare projector, in addition to the torpedo tubes.

opposite, bottom
Suitably stored and refuelled, warships can keep to the seas for extended periods, as the Americans proved during the Pacific war. Shown here is the ex-Victory class *Denebola* rigged for stores transfer.

below

The watchers watched. Permanent oil-production platforms in the North Sea are regularly monitored by Russian units suspicious of their true purpose. Here, a Natya-class minesweeper is, herself, observed by the purpose-built patrol ship H.M.S. *Orkney*.

refloated them and they were able to penetrate waters too hazardous for the parent craft.

This basic idea was used also in the more complex Landing Ship, Dock or LSD, a design which effectively reversed the LST, end-for-end, to confer better sea-going characteristics. They are best pictured as a self-propelled floating dock with a ship's bows and superstructure built over the forward end of the well and a stern gate in place of the bow doors and ramp. The American Ashlands were developed first, for which only reciprocating machinery was available which did not lend itself too well to being housed in the narrow side walls. Thus succeeding classes have all been steam turbine propelled, growing in size from the 4,800 light displacement of the 1944 Ashlands to the 10,000 tons of the latest Austin class. With their additional cubic capacity, the later ships have not only more accommodation for troops, but also vehicle decks forward. The minor landing craft need to return for more cargo, and the well can accommodate, typically, four 75-foot LCM 8s, each of which can carry a heavy tank or 60 tons of cargo. Floating pontoons can be carried by the LSD to act as a loading area alongside the ship, or linked end-to-end, a bridge for direct access to the shore. The after end of the docking well has a movable roof which can accommodate the operation of heavy helicopters. The superstructure is sufficiently large to house the personnel and communications necessary for the ship to act as a headquarters vessel if required, for overall control of an amphibious operation.

To date, the last word in assault ships are the Tarawa class at present being completed for the U.S. Navy. These are more like aircraft carriers in appearance, displace 40,000 tons when fully loaded, and can put ashore an oversized battalion with full mechanised support.

Besides the Americans, most other navies have an amphibious capability which is limited in size. The Russians, however, maintain a very large and versatile force.

A type of small warship formerly operated in large numbers by colonial powers was the River Gunboat. These are still maintained by countries such as Brazil, whose territory encompasses extensive rivers. The characteristics of the genre are a shallow hull, very boxy for the lightest possible draught, and with the accommodation raised in tiers above it, merchant ship style.

Several rudders are often incorporated to give the required rapid helm response for inland navigation.

The mine, as already noted, is not a new weapon but is probably the most cost-effective. The Russians used it in the Baltic during the Crimean War; Prime Minister Pitt saw demonstrations of it; the 'Torpedoes' damned by Dewey at Santiago were moored versions of it. Being invisible, its suspected presence was often enough to influence the movements of a fleet; when ignored, its effect could be catastrophic, examples being the British losses at the Dardanelles, from the 10th Destroyer Flotilla off the Dutch coast in 1917, and from Force 'K' from Malta in the Second World War.

Wide use of mines in both world wars caused not only losses but also the expenditure of much effort and manpower in establishing an auxiliary minesweeping force, largely from civilian fishing vessels. Fishing techniques, indeed, played a large part in the sweeping of the moored variety, which were laid both shallow to sink shipping and deep to sink submarines. As many of the latter disappeared without trace, the mines would appear to have been successful.

Minesweeping entered a new phase with the development of the influence mine. The principle of the magnetic mine was known to both the British and the Germans before the war, but the latter first made use of it. It was countered by 'de-gaussing' ships to reduce the magnetic 'signature' which triggered the mine. It was swept by using wooden minesweepers towing pulsed electrical sweeps.

The next development was the acoustic mine. As early designs were not too discriminating, their potential victims could usually explode them by means of an 'acoustic hammer', a device for generating noise and suspended

West German Schütze-class fast inshore minesweepers on an exercise. This type of ship is particularly valuable in countering the mine threat to shallow German offshore waters and estuaries.

West German corvette *Najade*, designed for anti-submarine operations inshore. Note the Bofors-type mortar forward.

above
The missile-carrying FAC poses a grave threat to larger warships operating in confined waters. The Penguin SSM being launched by this Norwegian Storm-class boat carries a 120kg war-head over 11 nautical miles and homes passively on to its target.

left
The British light fleet carrier *Triumph* was converted in 1958–65 to a fleet maintenance ship. She can now offer a wide range of repair facilities for RN units operating far from a conventional dockyard.

right
Best described as Helicopter Cruisers, the two Russian Moskvas are geared heavily to A/S work. In addition to their helicopter flight and A/S weaponry, they also carry A/A missile launchers and guns.

below
The short-ranged Seacat surface-to-air missile was designed to be a simple addition to small ships. This picture shows proving trials aboard H.M.S. *Decoy*, with an early-style open director.

below, right
In the Grisha class the Russians appear to have a successful design of corvette. They are gas-turbine propelled and visible are A/S launchers and SAM cover forward, torpedo tubes amidships, and 57mm guns aft.

from a conspicuous 'A' bracket in the bows. (This device is not to be confused with the 'foxer', towed by escorts to confuse acoustic torpedoes, which were tuned to home on to propeller noise). Multiple triggering devices were then installed, together with counters, which could be set to ignore a given number of stimuli, so that continuous sweeping was required to guarantee a safe channel.

The most dangerous type of all appeared in 1944 with the pressure mine, which exploded on the reduction of pressure caused by a ship's passage above it, i.e. the action of a land mine in reverse. As no satisfactory method has yet been invented of simulating this decompression field, the only safe method of sweeping is by countermining. The influence mine can be used in only comparatively shallow water so high-definition, sideways-looking sonars have been developed to

counter them that can detect any objects on the seabed. Any 'promising' contact is investigated either by divers operating from inflatable boats or, lately, by remotely-controlled vehicles such as the French PAP. The object of both is to place a small charge against the mine, which can then be detonated harmlessly. Although the Americans have tried sweeping mines by helicopter-towed sleds, their success rate both at Suez and Hanoi was rather less than satisfactory.

Specialist minelayers are somewhat rare vessels, maintained largely by countries such as Denmark and Turkey, which would wish to seal off a strategic waterway in time of war. Major navies tend to rely on the potential laying abilities of submarines, destroyers, aircraft, converted fast merchantmen and notably ferries.

Regular minesweepers progressed from the hybrid sloops of

1918 to metal-hulled craft such as the British Algerine class of 1942. Influence mines brought about the wooden ships, such as the American BYMs and the British MMS (known as the Mickey Mouse). Russia's expertise in mining brought about a vast building programme during the Cold War of the 'fifties, with several NATO navies building variations of the British coastal 'TON' and inshore 'HAM' designs. These are now over-age and the move is toward replacements constructed of GRP, or glass fibre. H.M.S. *Wilton* proved the technique and the new Brecons are following. Their changing methods are reflected in their change of classification from 'minesweeper' to 'mine countermeasures vessel' or MCMV. Another promising minesweeping craft is the large hovercraft, which is virtually immune to all types of mine.

Postscript

the future

When forecasting future trends, it is best to tread warily, for the pundit is all too often proved wrong. Without the impetus of war, the warship tends to develop cyclically, a simple concept gathering size and complexity with each succeeding class until it is elevated out of its prescribed original function and a new start is made. Thus, with the Nimitz and Tarawa classes, both the attack carrier and amphibious warfare ship have become so large and expensive that they are defeated by their own cost. With the era of STOL and helicopter, we may see a more modest amalgam of these two types.

Modern warships, epitomised by the Spruance and Perry classes, are geared to capacity rather than weight, having to accommodate extensive electronic systems. Both

Seabee Ship with Assault Landing Craft
1 LCM'S from lower barge deck, pre-loaded with heavy vehicles, being put afloat by lift
2 Roller system for transference of LCM's to lift at after end
3 LCM's on upper deck, pre-loaded with lighter vehicles, etc.

RoRo Ferry as Helicopter Carrier
1 Stern door retained for general use
2 Diesel uptakes discharge horizontally to reduce flight deck obstruction
3 Commercially available scissors lift to connect hangar and flight deck
4 Bow door secured

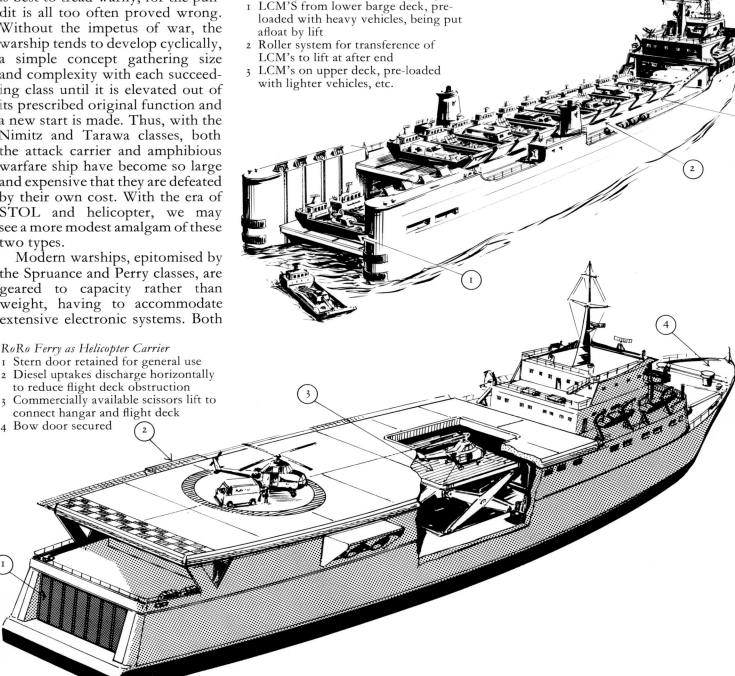

appear under-armed as they incorporate spare capacity for future installations, and this may be the first step toward the modular frigate, where a basic hull is designed to accept interchangeable modules containing varying weapon and control systems. This would enable the benefits of series production of hulls to be felt, whilst conferring flexibility in the rearming of ships for particular deployments.

Further introduction of nuclear power is likely to be slow unless a breakthrough is made in reducing size and initial cost, although these constrictions may well be ignored if a conventional fuel crisis develops. Surprises in such developments could be sprung by the Japanese, who are capable of great innovation in their warships. Their fleet is at present inhibited by its 'self-defence force' label.

It is difficult to see the submarine changing much from its present form although the means of countering it will improve, with submerged sensors permanently sited to track it, in conjunction with satellite observation. The airship may well have a future in A/S work; it is almost as fast as a helicopter, can carry a greater payload and hover almost indefinitely.

In spite of the enthusiastic statements of their respective lobbies, hydrofoils and surface-effect ships (hovercraft) are unlikely seriously to challenge the conventional warship outside 'sheltered' inshore waters. Their speed is bought at the expense of payload, and they are both complex and fragile; a warship should be able to absorb punishment as well as dispense it.

With the missile and its control systems becoming ever-more complex, their instant availability in a crisis and their resistance to action damage must be suspect. There is still a real place for the robust simplicity of the gun and developments in larger calibre, smooth barrelled weapons, automatically firing fin-stabilised projectiles, must be attractive, particularly when missiles can be jammed by ECM and decoys, requiring ECCM and more decoys to foil the anti-missile missiles. . . .

Natural slow evolution, however, would be upended by a real, shooting war. What is certain is that this will be over far too quickly to allow of any further construction and rival fleets will have to fight with what is available. As most western fleets are under-

strength, considerable reliance will have to be placed on the rapid conversion of high-quality mercantile tonnage during the build-up period.

Thus large container ships – some are over 800 feet in length and capable of over 30 knots – could be fitted with removable flightdeck panels over their forward hatches for the operation of STOL aircraft and helicopters. The facilities for these could be containerised to suit the ship, and space still be available for cargo if required.

Many large Roll-on, Roll-off ships and ferries need little more than having their various decks connected to the flight deck by scissors lifts rather than by ramps to produce fast escort aircraft carriers. Specialised tonnage such as Lash and Seabee ships need only to replace their cargo barges with LCM's to provide instant assault ships.

The possibilities are enormous but there is still no substitute for the purpose-built warship. The free world grew great in the past on a ready availability of them – it would be ironic if it were to collapse in the future through a lack of them.

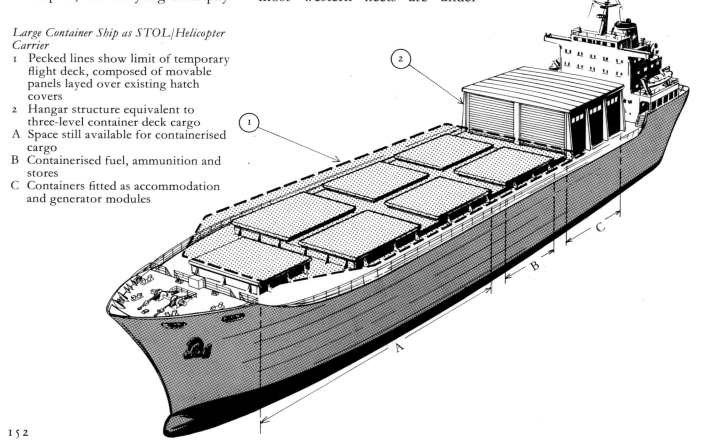

Large Container Ship as STOL/Helicopter Carrier

1 Pecked lines show limit of temporary flight deck, composed of movable panels layed over existing hatch covers
2 Hangar structure equivalent to three-level container deck cargo
A Space still available for containerised cargo
B Containerised fuel, ammunition and stores
C Containers fitted as accommodation and generator modules

Index

Acknowledgements

The lower illustration on page 45 is reproduced by gracious permission of Her Majesty the Queen.

The paintings and other items illustrated in this book are in the following collections: British Museum, London 11; Corpus Christi College, Cambridge (reproduced by permission of the Master and Fellows) 18; The Escorial, Madrid 25 bottom; Focke Museum, Bremen 21 top; Musée de la Marine, Paris 36 top, 41 top, 50 top; Museo del Ejército, Madrid 24 bottom; National Maritime Museum, London 21 bottom, 23, 27 top left, 28, 31 bottom, 31 top, 34, 35, 36 bottom, 37 bottom, 38, 39 top, 40, 42 centre, 42 bottom, 43 top, 44 bottom, 45 centre, 46 top, 48 bottom, 49 bottom, 51 top left, 51 bottom, 52, 54 top, 56 top, 57 bottom, 71, 74, 86, 89, 113; National Portrait Gallery, London 29 bottom, 45 top right; Nederlandsch Historisch Scheepvaart Museum, Amsterdam 24–25; Pepysian Library, Magdalene College, Cambridge (reproduced by permission of the Master and Fellows) 26; Rijksmuseum, Amsterdam 32; Science Museum, London 12 top, 14, 20, 44 top, 69 bottom; Smithsonian Institution, Washington DC 101; Southsea Castle, Portsmouth City Museums 53 bottom; Statens Sjöhistoriska Museum, Stockholm 45 top left; Universitetets Oldsaksamling, Oslo 16 right, 17 left; Chateau de Versailles 43 bottom.

Photographs:
Antikvarisk Topografiska Arkivet, Stockholm 16 left; Associated Press, London 100 bottom; Bavaria-Verlag, Gauting, Munich 75 top, 94 bottom, 97, 110 top, 120 bottom, 144 top left, 147 bottom, 148, 149 top; Bavaria Verlag – Fiore 15; Bavaria Verlag – Dr Herwig Happe 17 right; Bavaria Verlag – Knudsens Fotosenter 19; Bavaria Verlag – Hans Retzlaff 37 top; Chicago Historical Society 65 bottom; Corpus Christi College, Cambridge 18; Focke Museum, Bremen 21 top; Fujiphotos, Tokyo 96 centre; Photographie Giraudon, Paris 43 bottom, 50 bottom, 65 top; Hamlyn Group Picture Library 11, 21 bottom, 22 top, 22 bottom, 26, 29 top, 41 top, 41 bottom, 46 top, 53 bottom, 57 top, 62 bottom, 67 top, 67 bottom; Robert Hunt Library, London 47, 76 top, 77, 86 top; Image Press, London 87, 88, 103 bottom, 109, 115 bottom, 126 bottom, 143 top, 144 top right, 144 bottom, 149 centre; Image Press – Parker Gallery 50 bottom, 53 top, 55 top, 59, 62 top, 64, 76 centre, 76 bottom, 79 top; Imperial War Museum, London 60 bottom right, 61, 63 bottom, 66 top, 69 top, 69 centre, 70 top, 70 bottom, 72 top, 73 bottom, 75 bottom, 80 top, 81 bottom, 83, 84 top, 85 top, 85 bottom, 88 top, 88 bottom, 90 top, 92 top, 92 bottom, 93 top, 102 top, 103 top, 104 top, 104 bottom, 105, 108 bottom left, 108 top, 108 bottom right, 110 bottom, 114 top, 114 centre, 116 top, 116 bottom left, 117 centre, 119 centre, 122 bottom, 128 bottom, 141 top, 141 bottom, 142 centre, 142 bottom, 145, 147 top; Mariners Museum, Newport News, Virginia 51 top right; MAS, Barcelona 13, 24 bottom; Ministry of Defence, London 106 top, 106 bottom, 107 top, 107 bottom, 119 top, 120 top, 125 top, 125 bottom, 129 top, 129 bottom, 130, 136 top, 136 bottom, 139, 140 bottom, 146 top, 146 bottom, 147 centre, 149 bottom, 150 bottom right; Musée de la Marine, Paris 33 bottom, 36 top, 73 top, 78 top, 117 top, 121 bottom, 123 top; National Maritime Museum, London 23, 27 top left, 27 bottom, 28, 31 top, 31 bottom, 34, 35 top, 36 bottom, 37 bottom, 38, 40, 42 centre, 43 top, 44 bottom, 45 centre, 46 top, 48 top, 48 bottom, 49 top, 49 bottom, 51 top left, 51 bottom, 52, 54 top, 54 bottom, 55 bottom, 56 top, 56 bottom, 57 bottom, 58 bottom, 60 top, 60 centre left, 60 centre right, 63 top, 66 bottom, 71, 74, 81 top, 86 bottom, 89, 90 bottom, 93 bottom; National Portrait Gallery, London 45 top right; Nederlandsch Historisch Scheepvaart Museum, Amsterdam 24–25, 35 bottom; Novosti Press Agency, London 150 top; Orbis Publishing Ltd., London 138 bottom; Paul Popper Ltd., London endpapers 56–57, 58 top, 79 bottom, 82, 91, 94 top, 95, 96 top, 100 top, 115 top, 118 top, 118 bottom, 119 bottom, 121 bottom, 122, 124, 126 top, 127 top, 127 bottom, 128 top, 131, 132 top, 132 bottom, 133 top, 133 bottom, 134 top, 134 bottom, 135 top, 135 bottom, 137 top, 137 bottom, 138 top, 140 top, 143 bottom, 150 bottom left; Rijksmuseum, Amsterdam 32; Crown Copyright Science Museum, London 12 top, 12 bottom, 14, 20, 44 top; Science Museum, London 27 top right, 30 top, 33 top, 39 bottom, 69 bottom, 80 bottom, 84 centre, 102 bottom, 121 top; Smithsonian Institution, Washington DC 101; Statens Sjöhistoriska Museum, Stockholm 30 bottom, 45 top left; Universitetets Oldsaksamling, Oslo 16 right, 17 left; U.S. Bureau of Ships 78 bottom, 116 bottom right; U.S. Navy, Washington 84 bottom, 96 bottom, 99, 112, 117 bottom; Roger-Viollet, Paris 68, 72 bottom; Weidenfeld and Nicolson – Imperial War Museum 111; Weidenfeld and Nicolson – National Maritime Museum 39 top, 42 top, 42 bottom, 113.